Wild

Cats

of the

World

Wild
Cats

➤ of the ➤

World

Photographs and Drawings by

ART WOLFE

Text by

BARBARA
SLEEPER

Crown Publishers, Inc.

New York

To the many individuals—

artists, scientists, and ailurophiles—

who have been touched by the

spirit of the cat.

Published by Crown Publishers, Inc., 201 East 50th
Street, New York, New York 10022.
Member of the Crown Publishing Group.
Random House, Inc. New York, Toronto, London,
Sydney, Auckland

CROWN is a trademark of Crown Publishers, Inc.

Manufactured in Hong Kong

Design by Lauren Dong

Library of Congress Cataloging-in-Publication Data
Sleeper, Barbara.
       Wild cats of the world / text by Barbara Sleeper;
photographs and drawings by Art Wolfe.—1st ed.
       1. Felidae. 2. Felidae—Pictorial works. I. Wolfe,
Art. II. Title.
QL737.C23S5625   1995   94-28413

ISBN 0-517-79978-2

10   9   8   7   6   5   4   3   2   1

First Edition

Contents

Introduction

Four of us sat perched behind the enormous flapping ears of an Asian elephant. A small, barefoot mahout straddled the pachyderm's neck, prodding the great beast forward by means of weight shifts, soft verbal commands, and toe signals against the inside of the elephant's sensitive ears. So mounted, we rocked and lurched through tall elephant grass and across the Ramganga River of India's Corbett National Park.

We hoped to catch a glimpse of the mighty predator glorified by hunters, naturalists, and poet Rudyard Kipling: the big orange cat with black stripes—the tiger. As the five of us traveled alone through the forest and grassland habitat of the Himalayan foothills, all conversation ceased except for the occasional murmurings of the mahout. Around us was the mesmerizing spectacle of nature undisturbed.

Suddenly, amid this tranquillity, I saw it. Aglow in the late afternoon sun, a phantom orange shape appeared two hundred yards in front of us, at the edge of the shadowy forest. It was a large male tiger, the first tiger I had ever seen in the wild. Like a giant domestic cat, the tiger sprayed, then scratched in the sandy riverbank, pausing to sniff the ground. The majestic mammal moved slowly, deliberately, his dominance apparent even from a distance. The tiger's massive head, muscular shoulders and forelegs, and striking color seemed all the more impressive because he was wild.

Unaware of our presence, the tiger walked with an air of confidence and power I had not seen in any other animal. To observe a tiger without bars, to watch his natural behavior devoid of human influence, even for a moment, was a rare privilege. The encounter was intensified by our being perched atop another endangered species—the Asian elephant.

However, in an instant, the spellbinding sight ended. The tiger spotted us during a casual sweep of his keen yellow eyes. With a lightning transition from indolence to action, he spun and vanished into the forest.

I had a similar adrenalin-stirring encounter with a wild ocelot early one morning in the Cockscomb Basin of Belize. While walking the rain-forest trails in search of wildlife, I suddenly came upon the beautiful spotted cat as it boldly strolled the edge of the sanctuary's

Above: **The enormous ears of the African serval (** *Felis serval* **) are used to detect the quiet movement of rodents in tall grass. Once prey is located, this agile cat makes a high pounce to pin the unsuspecting creature with its front paws.**

dirt road. Immediately aware of my presence, the ocelot, unlike the tiger, calmly veered off the road without a change in stride. With unruffled dignity, he simply disappeared into the forest vegetation.

Travel over the years has left other images of wild cats etched across my memory: in Kenya, a leopard feeding at night in a tree; another briefly glimpsed walking by day through the grass at Lake Manyara National Park; lions on kills, resting in trees, and forever dozing; Asiatic lions tolerating the daily show of gawking pedestrian tourists in India; the intensity of a serval hunting in the African grass for rodents; the unperturbed, sphinxlike appearance of a caracal surrounded by tourist vehicles; the long-legged, tear-stripe elegance of a cheetah striding across the African savanna; and the insolent look of an Indian leopard camouflaged high in the fork of a tree.

Finally, I remember the vulnerability I felt on a foot safari in Zambia after a day stepping in elephant and antelope footprints—only to accidentally walk right into a pride of lions. The guide had an elephant gun with one bullet and a spare. We quietly backed away. That night, as we camped in the pitch black of Zambia's Luangwa Valley, the roaring of nearby lions, punctuated by staccato hippo grunts from the riverbank below, added Surround-sound to the campfire tales of man-eating lions and child-snapping crocodiles.

While writing this book, after a particularly intense day at the computer, I emerged from my office for a quick run to the post office. The first song that came on the car radio was "Sweet Lullaby" by Deep Forest, with jungle bird calls and a haunting tribal chant—and in the one and only car directly in front of me, in the middle of suburbia, a green parrot nibbled on the driver's ear. It was at that moment that I realized how pervasive the influence of rain forests, endangered peoples, and wildlife is on all of us—even in a distant city, even if only to cause an occasional subconscious stirring.

As the book was nearing completion, my nine-year-old son, David, suddenly announced one day that when he grows up, he is going to search for the lost dodo. He is sure that it is still alive someplace, and he is going to find it. When I asked him directly what he thought about all the stories and statistics he was hearing about lost rain forests and endangered wildlife, his response was immediate, and poignant.

A Masai Mara lioness (*Panthera leo*) exhibits the patience typical of all cat mothers. She allows a cub to sit on her back, as well as stick the extended claws of his left paw into her flank.

A puma (*Felis concolor*) photographed in Arizona demonstrates why this large feline is so difficult to see in the wild.

"It makes me very sad," he said. "Just think if animals treated us that way."

At the conclusion of nearly two years of living and breathing cats, of trying to synthesize an enormous feline literature that spoke of royalty and myth, humor and rapture—and, finally, endangerment—I had learned far more than I had anticipated, far more *from* cats than about them. Initially bemused by the thought of Egyptians building crypts to entomb a single mummified pet cat, complete with gold likeness and mummified mice to feed the pet during its journey to the afterlife, I grew to understand why the Egyptians had worshiped cats.

Throughout the history of man, cats have played an integral part in human culture. They have been life-saving in their ability to reduce rodent-caused food loss, disease, and pestilence. In paintings, poetry, and drama the enchanting feline image has reflected our cultural evolution in art, literature, and religion. At times revered, at others feared and hated, domestic cats have even mirrored the ever-changing status of women—as saint or seductress, as witch or maternal nurturer.

As we have become more and more estranged from nature and all things wild, domestic cats have been our consummate, uncomplaining companions, providing us with one of the most provocative bonds between man and animal, between civilization and untamed nature. From the beginning of recorded history, cats have served as guide and guardian to the spirituality of all things wild. They continue to do so now as they lie curled up on our twentieth-century hearths.

Learning about the hundreds and hundreds of people who are devoting their lives to the study, protection, and breeding of wild cats left me encouraged. The media is getting the message out about our need to conserve, recycle, and restore, to slow human reproduction and protect wild habitats. As dominant consumers, we have witnessed our devastating effects on the earth's resources. Now more than ever, it is time to join hands and hearts, and with hope, not blame, work together to stem the tide. It is time again to rejoice in the lessons of the cat.

BARBARA SLEEPER

1

Life as a Cat

CARNIVORE EXTRAORDINAIRE

[A cat is] an animal that is wary, watchful, stately, lordly, has glorious eyes and velvet paws and is, by all possible definitions, beautiful.

—ROGER CARAS, *A Celebration of Cats, 1986*

There is no mistaking a cat. "A cat is a cat is a cat," wrote e. e. cummings. From the world's largest feline, the Siberian tiger weighing up to 800 pounds, to the world's smallest, the rusty-spotted cat weighing just 2.2 pounds, from cats sporting spots to cats in tan coats—all felines are remarkably similar in design and function. They are quick, graceful, playful, and curious, with lithe bodies designed for the hunt. Scaled large or small, their size reflects their habitat and the prey they stalk.

Felines, or true cats, represent the highest level in the evolution of carnivores. They are meat-eaters whose lineage can be traced back more than 40 million years. Equipped with sharp teeth, strong jaws, retractable claws, and powerful leg muscles, cats are formidable predators designed to eat flesh. In between meals, they communicate with one another through an elaborate system of visual, vocal, and olfactory signals that delineate territory, announce sexual readiness, or warn of imminent attack.

Using excellent vision and hearing to detect movement, cats hunt by sight and sound. After a patient, calculated stalk, felines strike down their prey in a short rush. Their sharp claws and muscular, mobile forelegs enable these agile, quick-witted carnivores to climb trees, leap and swipe at birds, even cuff and grapple a wildebeest. Once cats are engaged with their prey, large canines grab and kill, hind claws can eviscerate, and the carcass is torn into swallowable chunks with scissor-sharp molars. Finally, small incisors and raspy tongues are used to scrape the very last morsels of meat from the bones.

Few people realize that there are thirty-seven different species of wild cats; fewer still that two-thirds of these species are now listed as rare or endangered, the rest as threatened. From snow line to sea level, arid desert to tropical rain forest, felines roam the wilds of planet Earth. While most species inhabit the temperate and tropical forests of the world, wild cats can be found on almost every continent. Yet no matter where they live, what they eat, how big or small, all cats are unmistakably alike. As stalking, hunting carnivores, felines represent the nearest thing to predatory perfection. Their successful evolution has filled the planet with cats.

Above: Like the majority of all wild cats, the oncilla (*Felis tigrina*), native to the Neotropics, is a secretive, solitary cat that stalks its prey at night.

Opposite: Near Kenya's Lake Nakuru, a female leopard (*Panthera pardus*) guards her prey, a warthog, in a tree.

Right: A leopard (*Panthera pardus*) is caught on a nocturnal prowl in South Africa's Londolozi National Park. Whether big or small, spotted, striped, or buff, there is no mistaking a cat. All felines appear as if designed from the same master plan.

Below: A rare black-footed cat (*Felis nigripes*) from southern Africa demonstrates the lithe, stretched-body stalk typical of most felines.

FELINE ARCHITECTURE

The ability to leap with agility and land with grace are two of a cat's most distinctive qualities. Felines can jump from trees, spring from ledges, slink like fluid along the ground, and make lightning pounces on unsuspecting prey. This movement is made possible by skeletons designed for maximum flexibility. Strong muscles and sinew hold a feline's bones together in a loose, supple package. This pliable structure gives a cat its grace and sinuous movement.

ened strides and to run fast by bringing its hind feet up in front of its front feet. Their specialized anatomy enables felines to maneuver narrow paths and squeeze through tight spaces.

A cat's ability to land on its feet is legendary. Experiments with domestic cats show that when dropped upside down from heights as little as one foot, alert cats can right themselves to land on all four paws in just 1.8 seconds. And once on the ground, all cats are digitigrade; that is, they elevate their feet to walk quietly on their padded toes.

Among the larger species—e.g., lions, tigers,

An extremely flexible spine enables a cat to turn and twist in pursuit of prey, arch its back in a half circle, move its legs laterally in sideswipes, and change direction in midair through hip rotation. Smaller cats can even curl up to sleep in a tight ball with their heads cradled on their shoulders. Shoulder blades positioned on the sides, rather than directly over the back, and reduced collarbones allow the lateral motion of the forelimbs. The accordion action of the backbone makes it possible for a cat to walk with length-

and leopards—much of the body weight consists of muscles. They lie in thick ropes and bands all over the animal's body. With forelegs as big as a man's thigh, tigers attack like battering rams to knock down prey weighing twice as much as they do. Following the kill, powerful jaw, neck, and chest muscles enable the big cats to drag heavy carcasses great distances—leopards hoist their kills up into trees.

While a cat's muscles enable it to move fast to subdue prey, they also enable a cat to move in

Many species of cats are agile tree climbers, such as this North American lynx (*Lynx canadensis*), perched high in a tree in British Columbia.

Above: A cheetah (*Acinonyx jubatus*), stretching on a termite mound in Kenya, illustrates the flexible feline backbone that enables this species to run like the wind, and others to leap, pounce, escape tight places—even curl up into a ball.

Right: A female ocelot (*Felis pardalis*) with kittens demonstrates the close tactile contact typical of felid mothers and young, as well as the anatomy that helps the kittens curl up at her side.

Opposite: In addition to having supple back-bones, all cats, such as this Eurasian lynx (*Lynx lynx*), are wrapped in muscles that enable them to move like fluid over the ground, freeze motion-less in an instant, and leap as if spring-loaded to overpower prey.

Above: As the larger spotted cats became endangered, poachers turned their attention to the smaller species of exotically marked felines, such as the ocelot (*Felis pardalis*).

Below: Despite their status as an endangered species, clouded leopards (*Neofelis nebulosa*) continue to be killed for their beautiful fur.

Although the how and why of feline coat coloration continues to be debated, one fact holds true. Spots and stripes have been the bane and glory of wild felines. Nothing works better to conjure up images of exotica—sex, wealth, and power—than the spotted coat of a cat. Nothing has been as coveted.

RETRACTABLE CLAWS

All cats have retractable claws that are used to climb, cut, hold, fight, and kill. In the cheetah, however, the claws remain visible even when retracted. Both sets of claws can be dangerous. A cat under attack will roll onto its back and rake with its hind claws to do serious damage. A lion can disembowel a zebra with the rapid delivery of a few convulsive kicks of its hind legs.

Feline claws are said to be the sharpest of all mammalian claws; the claws of the smallest cats have been likened to needle points. Each thick, hooked claw is attached by a ligament to the bone at the tip of each toe. Like stiletto switchblades, the front claws can be extended rapidly through a system of muscles, tendons, and elastic ligaments. When not in use, they are withdrawn into protective sheaths, which help keep them sharp. Cats sharpen their claws by raking them over rough surfaces like tree bark—or furniture—to strip off the old, dull claw sheaths.

Felines have five claws on the forefeet and only four on the hind feet. The first claw on the forefoot, which does not reach the ground, is called the dewclaw. Cheetahs use their dewclaws to seize and drag down prey. Lions use them to hook prey and dislodge pieces of meat too large to swallow. Arboreal cats such as leopards and margay use them to climb trees. In fact, the sharp and highly developed condition of the felid dewclaw indicates significant function.

Almost prehensile in their ability to grab, cuff, tap, hold, and snatch, a cat's front paws possess a versatility unique to felines. With lightning speed

Opposite: A cheetah (*Acinonyx jubatus*) sharpens its claws and leaves its scent on a tree trunk in Kenya's Masai Mara. It is one of the few species of wild cats whose claws remain visible even when retracted.

they can transform from touch-sensitive footpads used to tap a new object, groom, or elicit gentle social contact, to savage, lethal weapons. It is because of this dichotomy between languorous, inquisitive feline and cunning, calculating killer that cats are so intriguing. It is a dichotomy that can ultimately be measured by whether a cat's claws are in or out.

The pads on a cheetah's feet are part of its adaptation for speed. Tough and textured, they provide traction much as a tire does for a car.

A cheetah (*Acinonyx jubatus*) in Botswana's Okavango Delta shows off its lethal canines in a head-lowered threat posture that is typical of all cats.

CAT TEETH

A reduction in premolars and molars has led to a shortening of the jaw, a less protuberant muzzle, and the rounded head typical of all felines. Secured by powerful, highly developed jaw muscles, the joint between the lower jaw and skull is large enough to allow all cats to open their mouths as wide as necessary to kill their prey.

Cats have two sets of teeth from birth to death: a primary, or deciduous, set and their permanent teeth. They end up with either twenty-eight or thirty teeth, including four "fangs," or canine teeth, used to stab and hold prey during a kill. A gap or space behind each canine enables the cat to sink these teeth in as deep as possible during the killing bite, which is powerful due to the reduced length of the felid jaw. Cat canines are longer, stronger, and more cylindrical than those of dogs—and need to be when teeth hit bone.

Cats have twelve tiny incisors in front, used to pluck feathers and scrape meat from bones. The side teeth, or carnassials—the most scissorlike molars among carnivores—are used to shear through skin and muscle like knife blades. Articulation of the felid jaw permits use on only one side of the jaw at a time. This is the reason a cat bites a chunk of meat on one side of its mouth instead of in front as dogs and people do.

Left: Clouded leopards (*Neofelis nebulosa*) have the longest canine teeth in proportion to body size of any living cat, as shown in this skull. These weapons are used to subdue deer, wild pigs, monkeys, fish, civets, and occasionally domestic livestock.

Below: A lioness (*Panthera leo*) feeding on a buffalo kill in Botswana tears off a chunk of meat with her scissorlike carnassial teeth. Because all felines lack chewing and grinding molars, the piece of meat will be swallowed whole without chewing.

Cat tongues are covered with rasplike papillae that are used to scrape the last morsel of meat from bones. This yawning Bengal tiger (*Panthera tigris tigris*) displays not only his textured tongue, but the dagger-sharp canines used to force vertebrae apart in a death bite that can sever a prey's spinal cord.

Above: Three lionesses (*Panthera leo*) quietly drink from a water hole in Botswana's Okavango Delta, aided by their papillae-covered tongues.

CAT TONGUES

According to a French proverb, "he who licks can bite." Not only is this true of felines, but their lick can be as painful as their bite. An important part of a feline's feeding equipment is its tongue, which is covered with small hooklike projections called papillae. While a lick from a domestic cat feels rough, a lick from a lion's tongue will remove skin. The largest of the big cats can actually draw blood simply by licking the skin of an animal. Their raspy papillae are used to strip hair from hide and scrape meat from bones.

Cats rarely pant, and they also do not slurp and dribble when they drink water. Even when lapping liquids, cats are impeccably neat. Like miniature cups, felid papillae help hold fluids as the tongue is brought to the mouth.

Right: A black leopard (*Panthera pardus*) in South Africa curls its tongue during a languorous yawn. A cat's tongue is important for feeding, drinking, and grooming, and to make tactile social contact with other members of its species.

CAT GROOMING

All cats, big and small, have a distinctive way of grooming themselves with their tongues and forepaws, in a manner so ritualized as to be one of the most familiar images of a cat. Be they lions, leopard cats, or hearthside tabbies, all felines spend a considerable amount of time licking their fur and scrubbing their faces with their forepaws. Its supple spine enables a cat to stretch to lick and nibble almost every part of its body from the tip of its tail to its underbelly. The only places it can't reach with its coarse grooming tongue are its head, ears, and face. The cat solves this problem by dampening a forepaw with its tongue and then using it to scrub those tough-to-reach areas, particularly around its mouth after eating.

Opposite: An African cheetah (*Acinonyx jubatus*) grooms a littermate with its tongue. Such friendly tactile contact is thought to strengthen the social bonds between mother and young, littermates, and consorting pairs of amorous adults.

Above: A flexible backbone enables a grooming cat to lick and nip almost every part of its body, except the face. Here a leopard cat (*Felis bengalensis*) demonstrates how even this area is washed by first wetting a paw with its tongue.

Right: Whether a jaguar (*Panthera onca*) or a domestic cat, all cats spend a considerable amount of time grooming themselves—in a manner characteristic of all felines.

This elaborate grooming procedure does more than keep the fur clean. Licking helps remove unwanted odors and parasites from the coat. It also stimulates the skin glands to produce more body oils to waterproof the fur. And because only a cat's footpads can sweat, licking helps a cat stay cool through evaporation.

Felines use social licking to strengthen the bonds between individuals, particularly between mother and young, and consorting pairs. Domestic cats frequently direct this behavior toward their owners.

LANGUOROUS FELINES

Cats are accused of sleeping twice as much as other animals. They doze two-thirds of their lives away in a series of catnaps. This is certainly true for domestic cats left with very little else to do. However, wild cats are definitely energized when it comes to hunting, finding mates, and defending themselves. In between, they rest. One proposed explanation for this sleepy felid behavior is that cats tire easily because their lungs and hearts are small for their body size. A better answer may lie in the energy required to fuel a cat's muscles.

Capable of running at speeds of nearly seventy miles per hour, the cheetah (*Acinonyx jubatus*) is the world's fastest land mammal.

According to Michael Rogers (*National Wildlife*, October/November 1990), "Muscles are remarkable engines: extracting energy from the bloodstream, and then converting that energy into work—what physicists formally define as moving mass through a distance."

Muscles enable a leopard to chase a scrawny gerenuk across the Serengeti Plains, and a cheetah to run so fast that all four feet lift off the ground in an "aerial phase" that is both fast and energy efficient. They enable a caracal to leap four feet off the ground in a power arc to grab a francolin, and a domestic cat to crouch immobile by a bird feeder.

According to Rogers, a leopard's muscles are optimized for velocity. They are either moving very fast or not moving at all. Yet it requires energy just to walk and stand. Energy is burned even if the muscles are not moving. The energetics of feline locomotion, coupled with their intense stalk-and-ambush style of predation, probably explains why felines rest between bouts of hunting, feeding, fighting, and mating. In terms of energy efficiency, an isolated muscle expends about 25 percent of the energy it receives. Because smaller animals must move their limbs more often to cover the same distance, they are even less energy efficient than large animals.

Norman Myers observed the fact that a cat may lounge about for up to eighteen hours a day—and then transform into an efficient killing machine. "I sense there are several beings within one animal," he wrote (*International Wildlife*, November/December 1984), "and it is this sense of mystery about cats that has me hooked." Part of that mystery has to do with energy conservation.

The energetics of feline locomotion and predation, fueled by a strictly carnivorous diet, explains why felines rest between bouts of hunting, feeding, fighting, and mating. Among wild felines, no cat visibly seems to enjoy a siesta more than the lion (*Panthera leo*).

and tension around an impending murder by having the killer's silent stalk reflected in the watchful eyes of the victim's domestic cat.

More recently, Yuban coffee dramatically stalked customers in grocery stores by placing a photograph of a black leopard against a pitch-black background on the front of grocery carts. Below the glowering, yellow, ready-to-pounce felid eyes were the words, "Yuban, the spirit of coffee."

Cats, like humans and many species of primates—even owls—have forward-facing eyes. Not surprisingly, felines have the most highly developed binocular vision of all carnivores. When stalking prey, or jumping from branch to branch if arboreal, cats need to be able to judge distance accurately. Binocular vision with good depth perception makes this possible. Without moving their heads, cats can detect motion over a visual field of nearly 280 degrees, which includes roughly 120 degrees of stereoscopic vision straight ahead. For a forward-stalking predator, that is a significant portion of the

Above: The eerie eye shine of this Brazilian jaguarundi (*Felis yagouaroundi*) is caused by a special layer of reflecting tissue called the *tapetum lucidum*, which reflects back all external light.

Right: Photographed at night, a clouded leopard (*Neofelis nebulosa*) shows off one of the most haunting features of all cats—their eyes. With pupils dilated to the maximum, felines can see in the dark six times better than people.

CAT EYES

The cat's eyes are mysterious to us. More has been written about them than about the eyes of any other animal.

—ROGER CARAS, *A Cat Is Watching*, 1990

A cat's silent, intense gaze is both captivating and disquieting. The unintimidated, unblinking stare of a felid predator is one of power and intelligence. Unlike primates, which avert their eyes to avoid conflicts of hierarchy, cats don't look away. Visual contact between cats, directed at people and toward intended prey, can be intense. For this reason, it was believed that cats could read peoples' minds. The stare of a feline about to ambush its prey is particularly unnerving. There is no mistaking the cat's deadly intentions.

In "King of the Cats," poet Peter Porter captured the essence of a feline's eerie, glowing eyes when he wrote, "they burned low and red so that drunks saw them like two stars above a hedge." So universal are the human feelings generated by the seemingly emotionless stare of a cat that a filmmaker once effectively built suspense

visual field. Excellent peripheral vision enables them to detect movement from the sides. Their sensitive, rotational ears monitor movement behind them.

It is clear that cats analyze their environment and process information through their visual system. With wide, unblinking eyes, a cat does not make furtive glances from the corner of its eyes, but looks directly at an object. Because a cat's movements must be silent and precise, and its attack on prey deadly accurate, a cat will often move its head from side to side for a final assessment of distance before leaping.

"Midnight," wrote Thoreau, "is as unexplored as Central Africa to most of us." And so is the nocturnal domain of felines. To understand their world, one must enter the haunting realm of darkness. First comes dusk or civil twilight as the sun drops below the horizon; then comes nautical twilight when the brightest stars appear. Then comes night, when the faintest star becomes visible in the dark sky. It is during twi-

light that most felines are on the prowl. Yet, in Africa, only the telltale footprints etched in the dirt at sunrise allude to an abundant nocturnal presence—of hunting beetles, foraging hippos, hungry pit vipers, and stalking felines.

Typical of most nocturnal animals', felid eyes are large, an adaptation for night vision. In fact, cats have the largest eyes in proportion to body size of any carnivore, and can open their pupils to a maximum size three times greater than people can, letting in much more light. As a result, they need far less light to see than most other animals, and can see in light six times dimmer than humans can. Larger cats have round pupils, smaller cats distinctive vertical slits. During daylight, these dark-adapted pupils close down to tiny pinpricks and elliptical slits to protect the cat's eyes from bright glare.

To concentrate all possible light during the darkest of nights, felid eyes contain a layer of reflecting tissue behind each retina called the *tapetum lucidum.* This special membrane acts

At birth, many young cats have blue eyes, such as those seen on this caracal kitten (*Lynx caracal*) from South Africa. As they mature, their eyes take on the adult hues of green or amber.

Above and opposite:
All cats, including the small rusty-spotted cat (*Felis rubiginosa*) native to southern India and Sri Lanka, have a full set of whiskers. Not only are these tactile hairs used to enhance feline facial displays, but they serve as a guidance system that enables a cat to read objects and feel air currents, especially in the dark.

like a mirror to bounce scarce light back through the retina a second time for maximum stimulation. It is also what gives a cat it's all-knowing, all-seeing appearance, with deep, seemingly glass-marble eyes. Although one folktale holds that a cat's eyes glow at night by discharging light absorbed by day, in truth, a cat's eyes do not glow at all, but merely reflect back any light shined at them with their *tapetum,* in iridescent shades of blue-green, yellow-green, even red.

"Cats' eyes are splendid instruments," wrote Maitland Edey in *The Cats of Africa* (1968). "They can apparently focus clearly at any distance, from a few inches to infinity, their power of resolution is high and they are superb accommodaters.

One need only observe a cat intently watching a fly as it buzzes about a room to realize how good this accommodation is."

While it may seem that Egyptians let meowing cats vocally name themselves by calling them *mau,* the word actually covers two feline bases at once. In Egyptian, *mau* also means "to see," which cats do very well.

TACTILE CATS

Despite their reputation for being predominantly solitary, felid mothers with young, littermates, and amorous adults are extremely tactile. Lions seek and enjoy body contact with pridemates, rubbing heads and bodies together in greeting, often resting together in an indiscernible pile of tails, heads, and limbs. According to biologist George Schaller with the Wildlife Conservation Society of New York, the rubbing of body parts by one cat on another is an expression of friendliness.

One of the most sensitive organs of touch is a cat's whiskers. Thickened, tactile hairs are located on the upper lips, cheeks, chin, over the eyes, and on the inside of a cat's forelegs. These specialized hairs are deeply embedded in the tissue and supplied with nerve endings that transmit tactile information to the brain. While the more day-active, terrestrial cheetahs have reduced whiskers, the more arboreal, night-stalking leopards have some of the longest, most dramatic whiskers of any felid species, indicating their tactile importance during nocturnal forays on and off the ground.

Tapering to flexible, fine tips, whiskers function in the dark like a highly sensitive guidance system, enabling a cat to read objects and air currents much as the blind read braille. In effect, cats feel their way as they move, their whiskers giving the exact location of vegetation and other obstacles so a cat can move silently in the dark. During attack, the whiskers extend like a net in front of the mouth to help a cat assess the prey's body position and accurately deliver the lethal bite.

In fact, a cat's whiskers are nearly as motile and expressive as its ears, so much so that they are used to enhance feline facial displays. When a cat rests, they are extended to the sides. As a cat walks, they fan forward. When a cat is sniffing, greeting, or in a defensive posture, the whiskers are retracted to the sides. They even appear to wrap around the body of a rodent carried in a cat's mouth—ready to detect a last twitch.

CAT NOSES

Although canines hold title in the sniff-and-smell category, cats also have an excellent, often underrated sense of smell. Cook a chicken, and a domestic cat will disrupt a deep sleep to hang around the kitchen. Place a dish of food on the floor, and a "finicky" cat will smell first before sampling. Bring a new object into the house, and a domestic cat will be over in an instant to investigate this intrusion into its territory—by carefully smelling it.

From thoughtfully smelling an owner's breath to sniffing the lingering scent left behind by a strange pet, domestic cats spend a considerable amount of time smelling the airways. In fact, if you watch how a domestic cat moves in the garden, you will see that it spends a great deal of time in tail-up, nose-close smelling, often rubbing or rolling in scents it finds most appealing. One of those scents is dried catnip, which can set a

An Asian golden cat (*Felis temmincki*) from Southeast Asia gives an unmistakable visual warning display. All cats have a good sense of smell which is used to detect a wide range of feline olfactory signals.

This Brazilian pampas cat (*Felis colocolo*) has a very distinctive nose. Like human fingerprints, the nose pads of cats differ by individual, with no two alike.

normal cat aquiver with rolling, rubbing, and head-shaking.

The sense of smell is even more important to wild cats, who must find food and mates, defend territories, and avoid predators. Felines use the sense of smell to read the scent messages left behind by other cats as well as by their prey.

CAT EARS

"Cats are victims of their own senses," wrote D. J. Bruckner in *Van der Steen's Cats* (1984). "They cannot turn their ears completely off, or their noses for that matter. A recumbent cat, sound asleep, will suddenly shoot off in a flying leap at things no other animal senses, sometimes at nothing, and once it is on the move it is almost impossible to distract."

Not only do cats have an acute sense of hearing, up to fifty thousand cycles per second, but their mobile, radarlike ears can be quite expressive. With each ear controlled by more than twenty muscles, cats can rotate each one nearly 180 degrees, covering most of a 360-degree sound field without even moving their heads. Like the movement of a chameleon's independent eyes, one feline ear can swivel back while the other points forward. In fact, a cat's ears move so instinctively to pinpoint sound that a keen observer can visually follow them to gain directional clues.

Not only are cats' ears constantly moving, but they also change shape to signal the emotions of their owner. When a cat is asleep, or relaxed, its ears are rounded and point forward and out, to broadly screen sounds. When the ears become erect and point straight ahead, they signal that the cat is alert and staring at something. Sometimes a cat's ears will twitch and quiver rapidly in rhythm to its chattering vocalizations. This indicates the cat is agitated and tense, such as when it sees a bird or mouse, but is unable to get within stalking distance.

Opposite: Like Stealth bombers, cats such as this snow leopard (*Panthera uncia*) utilize every sensory means possible to locate prey and avoid detection. Moving like mobile radar units, a cat's ears are especially sensitive to the slightest noise, and they can move independently of each other to detect it.

A cat's ear flaps are delicate. To protect them when frightened or anticipating attack, a defensive cat will flatten them against its head, making them nearly invisible when viewed from the front. This ear posture gives the cat a bizarre, rounded-head appearance—an effective signal that the cat is frightened and ready to defend itself. Should a cat become aggressive without fear, the ears will rotate backward, but not flatten. The backs of the ears become visible from the front—a warning signal that the cat will attack if further provoked.

Much has been written about the stimulating effect of movement on the cat's predatory instincts. Yet, like bat sonar, the sensitive, fluttering ears of a margay, constantly quivering, turning, and twitching to high-pitched sounds inaudible to our ears, indicate just how important hearing is to cats. How else could they hear the quiet footsteps of mice?

Above: The enormous tufted ears on this South African caracal (*Lynx caracal*) are used not only to detect prey, but to convey its moods and intentions in a series of ritualized facial displays.

Right: This tiny black-footed cat (*Felis nigripes*), native to southern Africa, is mad enough to attack. The ears, flattened and twisted so the backs are visible from the front, signal its aggressive mood and intention.

EAR SPOTS

"For a while, the black spots on the backs of their ears can still be seen among the waving grass as the lionesses deviate more and more to the left, but eventually all three vanish as completely as if they had been swallowed up by the earth," wrote C. A. Guggisberg in *Wild Cats of the World* (1975).

Many people have mused over the significance of the distinctive white ear spots seen on several species of cats, such as the tiger, margay, ocelot, and clouded leopard, and the black ear spots seen on the lion. Among lions, the black tail tip and black-backed ears stand out from behind, helping pride members stay in touch as they crouch and stalk through lion-colored grass. They also help the cubs follow adult movement.

Eight-year-old Ben Jamieson of Arlington, Virginia, winner of a *ZooGoer* PawPrints Animal Facts Contest, explains it best. "Some female big cats have a large white spot on the back of each ear. It looks like a headlight

Above: The little-known marbled cat (*Felis marmorata*), native to Southeast Asia, illustrates how visually dramatic white ear spots can be on an otherwise cryptically colored cat. Not only do they help signal their owners' emotions, but they serve as beacons for the young to follow.

Left: Felid ears are extremely mobile and expressive. Their signaling capability is further enhanced by the eye-catching black ear tufts, or black or white spots typically located on the back of each one—such as the flaglike white bars on the ears of this serval (*Felis serval*).

when the babies are following behind their mother and helps them keep sight of her."

Desmond Morris (*Catwatching,* 1986) had his own ideas. "The aggressive ear posture has led to some attractive ear-markings in a number of wild cat species, especially the tiger, which has a huge white spot ringed with black on the back of each ear. When a tiger is angry, there is no doubt at all about its mood, as the pair of vivid white spots rotates into view."

CAT TAILS

Except for the stubby-tailed lynx and bobcat, and the tailless Manx, most cats have long tails. The distinctive appendage serves as a visual gauge of its owner's emotions—lashing back and forth in anger, held high in a question mark during greetings and exploration, tucked low when frightened or during attack, the tip twitching excitedly as prey draws near. Other times it simply droops over a branch reflecting the relaxed dominance of its resting owner.

Most familiar is the expressive tail of a house cat, held upright as it rubs against its owner's legs or when the cat runs to its dinner plate. Domestic cats seem to have an almost prehensile ability to nonchalantly run their tail over one's feet, or leave it resting across one's toes, making ever so subtle, but direct, physical contact.

Cat tails produce highly effective, low-energy signals. Distinctive markings such as rings, black tips, and white tips accentuate the visual messages conveyed when a tail is lowered, raised, or lashed from side to side. Cheetahs and other species have white-tipped tails, or tails with white

Feline tails can function as balancing rudders, such as when snow leopards (*Panthera uncia*) climb and leap onto rock outcroppings in their native high-altitude habitats—or chase each other in playful abandon as rambunctious juveniles.

or pale undersides, which are exposed when the tips are curled above the ground. Paul Leyhausen suggested that such markings may help kittens follow their mothers in the dark, or through tall grass.

Other species key into these signals as well. While photographing leopards in South Africa's Londolozi National Park, Art Wolfe watched a male leopard hunting, its tail down. When birds spotted the stalking cat, they harassed him so badly with alarm calls that he gave up. He immediately raised his tail, white tip waving back and forth—and the birds stopped calling.

Long tails also help cats balance. The cheetah uses its tail like a rudder to switch direction during high-speed chases after zigzagging antelope. Arboreal species, such as clouded leopards and margays, use their tails during acrobatic leaps and for walking along branches in the jungle canopy. And tails are used for balance during ambush pounces on prey. Among smaller species, cats even use their tails as paw muffs, curling them neatly around their front feet when they rest.

Lacking long tails, lynxes and caracals appear to use their ear tufts as signaling replacements. Caracals use their black-tufted ears in elaborate head-flagging displays. Feline specialist Andrew Kitchener proposes that the jungle cat, with a short tail and slight ear tufts, may represent an intermediate stage in the shift from tail to ear communication.

Adept at conserving energy, felines utilize subtle movements of their tails to convey mood or intention. White or black tips help draw the eyes to these posterior signals and are thought to help cubs keep track of their felid moms as they move through vegetation. Here a leopard (*Panthera pardus*) raises the conspicuous white underside of its tail.

THE CAT'S MEOW

Cats are extremely vocal. In addition to their distinctive body language, accentuated facial expressions, and mood-signaling tails and ears, cats are credited with making at least twelve different vocalizations, from meows, screams, and roars to chirps and twitters. Anyone who has been awakened to the night-piercing wail of a prowling tomcat knows how expressive a feline voice can be—and who hasn't jumped at what sounded like the cry of a distressed human infant, only to discover it was produced by a cat.

Gustav Peters, in *Great Cats* (1991), identified three types of low-intensity reassurance or greeting vocalizations in cats that each lasts less than half a second—gurgling, prusten, and puffing. Lions and leopards "puff" in what sounds like an attack of muffled sneezing. Tigers, snow leopards, jaguar, and clouded leopards "prusten," that is, make a sound like that of a snorting horse. Other felid species "gurgle," producing a sound combination that resembles a cooing pigeon and a babbling brook.

Get a cat really upset, and it will spit, hiss, and growl. It has been suggested that, much like an eye-spotted moth mimicking a fearsome predator, a spitting, hissing cat, with its ears flattened against its round head and its tail whipping back and forth, is mimicking a snake about to attack.

"We know as much about how the great stars form, operate and die as we do about a cat's purr," wrote D. J. Bruckner in *Van der Steen's Cats* (1984).

While no accurate record exists of which species can and can't purr, enough species do to make this a characteristic feline trait. This universal sound of contentment is typically produced at close range, between a mother cat and her young. While cats probably purr by vibrating two folds of skin that lie behind their vocal cords, no one knows for sure. If the vibrating is caused by breathing air in and out, why doesn't the tone change with each breath? Kittens can purr while nursing; adult cats can purr and produce other vocalizations at the same time.

Above: White rings around the eyes, white stripes running down either side of the nose, and white markings on the cheeks, chin, and mouth help accentuate facial displays made by the leopard cat (*Felis bengalensis*) of Southeast Asia.

Below: With oversized eyes in hues of green or gold, often highlighted with spots and stripes, felid faces can be visually dramatic. Such is the case with the bobcat (*Lynx rufus*). When two armed, contesting felines meet, the face-to-face, eye-to-eye contact can be intense. It is best if each can quickly read the other's intentions in order to avoid battle.

Opposite: The cryptically colored tiger (*Panthera tigris*) relies on its vertical black stripes to break up its telltale body outline. Yet its face is highlighted in dramatic white, from white eye rings and eyebrow patches to white cheeks and chin, which blend into a black-and-white-striped chest. The facial markings on each tiger are unique to that individual.

Above: A bobcat (*Felis rufus*) sprays urine on a tree branch to create a chemical signpost for all that follow. Such chemical messages are used by felids to delineate territorial boundaries as well as to convey sexual status.

SCENT OF A CAT

In addition to vocalizations, facial expression, and body language, cats also communicate with one another via chemical signals. They accomplish this through the production of long-distance-acting hormones, or pheromones, and by chemical messages left in their feces and urine.

Cats are loaded with scent glands. They are located around the mouth, cheeks, chin, and anus, between the toes, and at the dorsal base of the tail. Scents produced from these glands are used to mark territorial boundaries, signal sexual readiness, and maintain social bonds between mothers and young, among lion pridemates, and between domestic cats and their owners.

Cats leave their odoriferous scent trails wherever they lie down, and when they walk, scratch tree trunks, or scrape the ground with their hind feet. They scent-mark territorial landmarks and

Below: All cats are equipped with a special vomeronasal organ called the Jacobson's organ, located on the roof of their mouths. This male snow leopard (*Panthera uncia*) is using his in a *flehmen* response to taste-smell the intoxicating sexual message of a female in estrus.

those they are most intimately associated with by rubbing them with their heads, cheeks, and bodies. To convey the sexual messages contained in urine, both sexes scent-mark with this body fluid. Males use their retractable penises to spray urine backward onto bushes, trees, posts, walls, even people—at nose level, wherever other cats may pass.

Dominant animals typically scent-mark more often than subordinants. Dominant male cats have been known to deposit their feces in prominent locations, while females with young often bury theirs to avoid detection. Male lions typically head-rub an object, spray it with urine, and then scrape nearby. Such actions leave several different visual and olfactory messages, including the visually conspicuous and smelly one of sprayed urine.

Because scent-marks fade, they have to be continually updated along territorial borders. In the process, all rival marks are eliminated in a chemical arms race among males to protect both their territory and access to females. To transfer some of the scent to the animal producing it, cats will rub their heads against urine marks, or scrape feces and urine with their hind legs.

A female cat in estrus will also spray urine. Olfactory changes in the female's glandular secretions and urine announce that she is in heat. This is one of the most important chemical messages a male needs to read.

To help smell such intoxicating scents, all felids have a special vomeronasal organ called the Jacobson's organ located in the roof of the mouth, which makes it possible for a cat to simultaneously taste and smell the olfactory messages left by other cats. The sexual message in urine from estrous females is so powerful that when a male detects this intoxicating scent with his Jacobson's organ, he stares, wrinkles his nose, curls his upper lip, and grimaces with an open mouth in what is called the *flehmen* response. Because estrus lasts just a few days, time is of the essence. The female's sexually motivating sensory messages, received through the Jacobson's organ, help males find their mates.

Right: **A South African leopard (*Panthera pardus*) takes time out to read the olfactory messages left by other leopards on this chemical signpost. All cats spray their urine at nose level.**

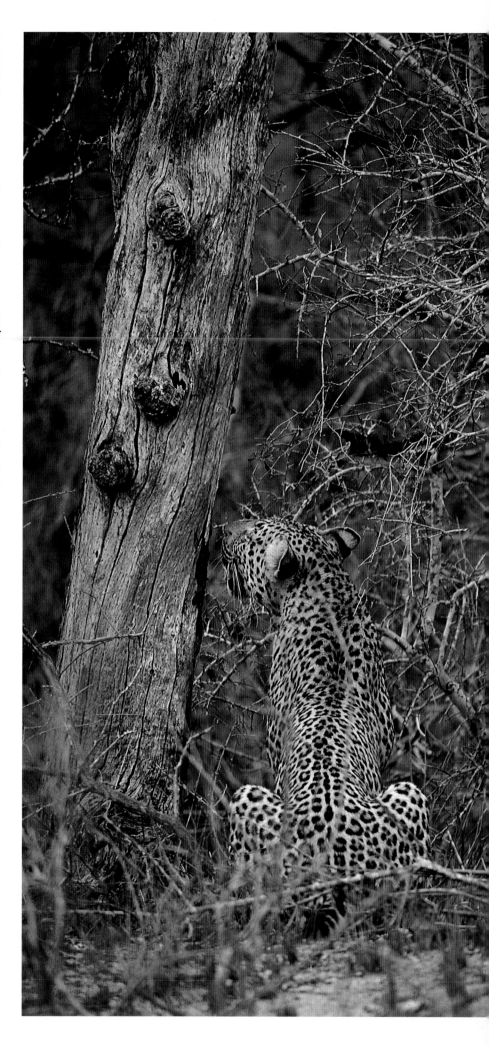

CAT FIGHTS

Ignorant people think it's the noise which fighting cats make that is so aggravating, but it ain't so—it's the sickening grammar they use."

—MARK TWAIN

Cats are polygamous, which means they have more than one mate. As a result, males must compete with one another for access to receptive females and their territories. Several female territories often overlap with one male's home range. Male competition for sex and turf can lead to hissing, spitting catfights. Rival males sometimes fight to the death.

For example, competition for limited cheetah territories on the Serengeti Plains is especially intense. According to wildlife biologist Tom Caro from the University of California, Davis, who studied the Serengeti cheetahs, so many males have been killed that the adult sex ratio there has been skewed one-to-two in favor of females. Coalitions of males have greater success at acquiring and holding territories because they are better able to fight off rival males. Even so, fights can be nasty. Males die when they are pinned down by an opponent who then secures a suffocating neck bite. Once the victim is down, coalition partners join the fray to bite at the haunch and genitals of the vanquished male.

Few male lions survive much past twelve years of age, due to the intense competition over access to female prides. Even if a male coalition succeeds in gaining control of a pride, their tenure is usually short-lived. There is always a rival coalition waiting to take over.

ROUGH SEX

Once a female signals her receptivity with tantalizing chemical messages, the males gather. "It is

Opposite: **Although lions (*Panthera leo*) are normally found on the ground throughout their African range, a few occasionally take to the trees to rest in the shade. Here two playful Serengeti lions visually joust in a tree.**

then," wrote Roger Caras in *A Celebration of Cats* (1986), "that the female is at her alluring best, when she enters her often noisy courtship stage and sends all the males around her into a tizzy of anticipation—with volunteers up and down the block."

Feline courtship can be prolonged, with a great deal of visual and vocal communication between partners. At first the female rebuffs the male with extended claws, growls, and spits—but as estrus progresses, her behavior becomes more solicitous. She vocalizes, rubs against objects, and seductively rolls and stretches. As courtship

Below: **While courting or fighting, feline confrontations can be visually and vocally dramatic, characterized by intense staredowns. Two leopard cats (*Felis bengalensis*) native to Southeast Asia lock eyes on a branch.**

Male lions break all
records for sexual
athletics. During a
female's five-day estrus,
a dominant male will
often mate with her
every twenty to thirty
minutes for hours
at a time.

progresses, these behaviors are directed toward a prospective mate. Tactile contact becomes especially heightened during courtship. Males become attentive and possessive and fend off rival males.

All cats are induced ovulators—that is, the female must be stimulated through copulation before she will ovulate, and only then can the eggs be fertilized. To that end, male cats are endowed with penis bones or bacula that come in species-specific shapes and sizes. The tip of the penis is often covered with sharp keratinous spines, like a porcupine, all pointing ventrally. Ovulation is probably triggered during copulation by the intense pain caused when the male withdraws his spiny appendage. Therefore, the more frequently a male mates with a female, the greater the chance he has of inducing ovulation and fertilizing her eggs.

Male lions hold the record for sexual athletics. During the five-day estrus, dominant males have been observed mating every twenty to thirty minutes, for hours at a time, with their receptive partner. One male lion observed by George Schaller copulated with two females 157 times in fifty-five hours. However, as soon as the period of estrus ends, so does the romance and the male is gone.

Feline sex can be rough. Mating males typically bite the back of the female's neck, sometimes seriously enough to draw blood. They do this to mimic the calming, neck-carrying bite of a mother cat. This buys a male time and a bit of protection during copulation. Even so, both cats are vulnerable. Neither can afford to be injured, so courtship amounts to a laying down of arms long enough to copulate. At the conclusion, the female often cries out—whether due to the withdrawal of the backward-facing spines, or as a means to achieve a quick, safe distance from a strange male, no one knows for sure. In the end, a female cat, or queen, is only receptive for a few intense days, then males and females go their separate ways.

Because most felines are solitary, courtship rituals can be prolonged as a strange male tries to get close enough to a female to safely mate. Neither wants to get mortally wounded in the process. Lions, however, with their pride social structure, are somewhat of an exception.

COMBO-CATS

Studies of feline genetics have revealed a basic similarity in felid chromosomes, so much so as to make crossbreeding between certain species possible. Under normal conditions, species-specific reproductive behavior coupled with geographic barriers prevents most hybridization from occurring in the wild. However, in a few labs and zoos, experimental genetic crosses have been attempted. Among the larger cats, ligers (male lion and female tiger), tigons (male tiger and female lion), and leopons (lion and leopard) have been created. Crosses between jaguar and leopard, puma and tiger, lion and jaguar, and jaguar and puma have also been achieved. Typically the progeny from such crosses have been sterile. Among the smaller species, the domestic cat has been crossed with bobcats, black-footed cats, oncillas, and leopard cats. Bobcats have been crossed with ocelots.

Unwanted hybridizations have occurred in the wild when free-roaming feral house cats have bred with the European wildcat, African wildcat, and the jungle cat—resulting in fertile offspring. Such crosses further weaken the integrity of the gene pools of species that are vulnerable. Because feral cats can produce up to three litters a year, and most wild cats only one, endemic species can quickly lose ground to feral cats that invade their habitat.

CAT MOTHERS

The main social grouping among most species of cats is between the mother and her young. Males and females almost never form pair bonds, except temporarily to mate. Feline family life is affectionate and intimate. As teachers and protectors, feline mothers are patient with their romping, playful young.

Feline moms typically give birth in secluded places, away from commotion. The young are born live, blind, and helpless. They cuddle together while the mother goes off to hunt. Most females raise their cubs without male assistance, except for the lion. In the Serengeti, George Schaller observed males sharing prey with cubs—after stealing it from the females.

The energetics of female reproduction are

Opposite: **A female cougar (** *Felis concolor* **) stands guard over her two cubs. As predators in training, the cubs accompany their mother to learn and explore their environment and become familiar with prey by sharing her kills.**

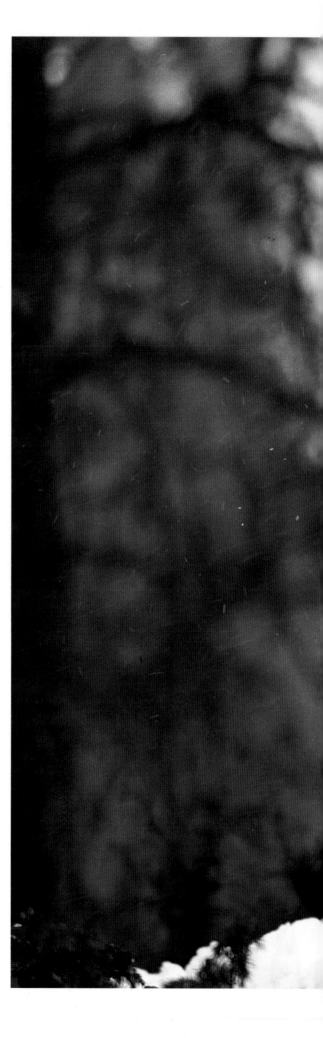

it. This is accomplished by exposing the young to a variety of prey at mealtime, by releasing live prey in front of the cubs during organized practice sessions, and by letting them accompany their mother on hunting forays.

In the wild, felid mothers pick up their kittens by the loose skin at the backs of their necks and move them to new den sites if they sense danger. In captivity, they will kill, cannibalize, or abandon their young if something is wrong. According to small-felid specialist Pat Quillen, director of SOS Care, Inc., in Valley Center, California, if the mother is stressed, her kittens are at risk. It is imperative that the female feel safe and secure in order to raise her young successfully. "When you see a mother carrying her young and pacing about," says Quillen, "you immediately know that there is a problem."

And for many rare and threatened species of small felids, there is a problem, as few are easy to maintain in captivity, much less breed.

FELID PLAY BEHAVIOR

All cats play. They play with other cats, with living and dead prey, with inanimate objects, and by themselves. Mother cats play with their young. Mates play during courtship. Through play, juveniles train for intraspecific aggression and learn predatory skills such as the species-specific cheetah paw slap, margay hind-foot push, and lion leg swat and flank tackle.

According to Swiss zoologist Rudolf Schenkel, the play activity itself expresses tenderness and fondness. Pawing, seizing with jaws, licking, and other apparently pleasing body contact show the same fondness as the suckling scene. Play also contains elements of stalk and ambush, attack and fight, and escape and pursue—the precursors of life as an adult carnivore.

A kitten inviting a littermate to play widens its eyes and presses its ears forward. The invitation may include a stalk and pounce, or an arched back. With tail curled, it may sidestep toward or around a playmate, then roll onto its side and hold its tail in a hooked position.

In his book *Animal Play Behavior* (1981), author Robert Fagen addressed what he calls the biological paradox of play. "Why," asked Fagen, "do young and old animals of many species spend time and energy, even risk physical injury, to play?"

Research has shown that nearly 90 percent of all cheetah cubs born in Tanzania's Serengeti National Park die within the first three months of life. Predators such as hyenas, jackals, lions, and birds of prey account for half the cub mortality. Cheetah mothers will abandon their cubs if they cannot kill enough prey to fuel the energy demands of hunting and lactation.

quite extraordinary. Female cats have the heavy energy demands of gestation and lactation, coupled with the energy expenditure—and risk—of hunting for food to provision their young. While in search of food, they risk losing their reproductive investment to predation or, in the case of lions, to infanticidal males.

While lying on their sides to nurse their young, females will often wrap their tails around the kittens and put a paw over them to protect them and keep them warm. Not only do felid moms nurse their young, share their kills, and show incredible patience supervising their playful kittens, but also, in age-appropriate stages, they teach their offspring how to become efficient carnivores—which prey to attack and how to kill

An ocelot kitten (*Felis pardalis*) practices a neck bite on its mother while its sibling goes for a flank hold. Such play behavior will later be used to subdue prey and reconnoiter prospective mates.

Above: Young snow leopards (*Panthera uncia*) playfully tackle each other. Such behavior is characteristic of highly intelligent animals and is used to help practice skills needed as adults. Among felines, play behavior has been perfected to a fine art.

FELINE OLYMPICS

When it comes to breaking athletic records, many members of the cat family could win gold. The long-legged cheetah holds the land-speed record, reaching 68 miles per hour from a standstill in mere seconds. The thirty-five-pound caracal or desert lynx is also a fast sprinter for its size. Quick and agile, this small cat can leap high into the air to knock down low-flying birds—and kill several pigeons in a flock before the rest take flight.

Cougars are jumping specialists, using their powerful hind legs to leap distances of twenty feet or more. Leopards are also skilled at leaping, often out of trees to ambush prey. The small margay of Central and South America ranks high as an aerial gymnast. As it dangles upside down from a branch by one hind foot, its specially designed ankle bones allow 180-degree rotation. These dextrous ankles also enable margays to climb headfirst down tree trunks.

But when it comes to all-round feline prowess, the tiger shows the most remarkable athletic talent. Tigers can walk eight to fifteen miles in a night. At an extended run, they can clear thirteen feet in a bound and can leap twenty-three feet or more. As the largest of all cats, tigers are strong enough to attack bears, steal carcasses from crocodiles, and drag a dead, 400-pound buffalo a third of a mile. Equally adept at swimming, the notorious man-eating tigers of India's Sundarban swamps have boldly swum out to attack people in boats.

SMART CATS

"I have not the slightest notion what goes on in the mind of my cat Jeoffry," wrote Lewis Thomas (in *Audubon,* March/April 1992),

Right, above and below: With the signaling function of their white ear spots clearly visible, a mother tiger (*Panthera tigris*) play-wrestles with her cub.

Opposite, below: A nearly full-grown leopard (*Panthera pardus*) playfully socializes with his smaller mother. Soon she will abandon him, leaving him equipped with the skills he will need to survive.

Cougars (*Felis con-color*) are built to leap in and out of trees, and navigate with great speed and agility through steep canyons and ravines. Their long hind legs, much longer than their forelegs, enable them to do this.

"beyond the conviction that it is a genuine mind, with genuine thought and a strong tendency to chaos, but in all other respects a mind totally unlike mine. I have a hunch, based on long moments of observing him stretched on the rug in sunlight, that his mind has more periods of geometric order, and a better facility for switching itself almost, but not quite, entirely off, and accordingly an easier access to pure pleasure. Just as he is able to hear sounds that I cannot hear, and smell important things of which I am unaware, and suddenly leap like a crazed gymnast from chair to chair, upstairs and downstairs through the house, flawless in every movement and searching for something he never finds, he has periods of meditation on matters I know nothing about."

Talk to any cat lover, and you will be regaled with tales about how intelligent his or her feline pet is. There are cats that can open and close doors, cats that play fetch and rousing games of hide-and-seek, cats that prefer privacy when using the loo, and cats that shun kitty litter for human toilets, even flushing them after use.

One such smart, toilet-flushing cat in Corvalis, Oregon, was recently accused of impacting his owner's water bill. According to an article in the *Seattle Times* (March 31, 1993), in one month,

Maurine Steinauer's bill jumped $29.50, or three thousand gallons—an increase of nearly 50 percent. After the utility company told her the higher bill reflected an increased use of the toilet, she kept the bathroom door shut while at work. Sure enough, with the feline flusher's access thwarted, Steinauer's bill dropped along with the water use.

There is no doubt that wild cats are smart. Their elusive behavior in the wild is one indication. Another is their successful stalk and ambush hunting technique, based on the careful observation and anticipation of prey behavior. Equally significant is the haunting ability of tigers, leopards, and lions to ocassionally turn these predatory skills on people—boldly stalking and snatching *Homo sapiens* from the midst of civilization.

All carnivores are intelligent—they have to be in order to outwit their prey. To survive, they must be smarter than the animals they hunt. An interesting example is the octopus, notorious as both predator and escape artist. Octopuses have such highly developed brains that the smaller species are said to rival mammals, *such as cats,* in terms of intelligence. Like the octopus, most felines (except for lions and occasionally mothers with cubs) hunt solo. They must be smart, skilled, and well armed in order to kill prey by themselves.

Masters of their territory, smart cats learn the game trails, memorize the feeding and resting habits of their prey, and know the best places to hide in ambush. Before making a premeditated attack, they patiently study the terrain and calculate the direction of the wind. Often they wait for that precise moment when an unsuspecting victim is most preoccupied with feeding, fighting, mating, or playing to make their attack. In effect, felines are animal behavior experts. They quietly observe the habits of their prey in order to break down their defenses.

As it turns out, when a cat has only its food bowl to stalk, weight problems aren't the only by-product of domestication. In a study of cat brains conducted by Robert Williams of the University of Tennessee at Memphis and Carmen Cavada and Fenando Reinoso-Suarez of the Universidad Autonoma de Madrid, it was found that the brain of *Felis catus* is shrinking. By comparing the brains of adult domestic cats to those of adult Spanish wildcats—a living relative of the hearth-side tabby—they found that domestic cat brains were 20 to 30 percent lighter. During the course of evolution to domesticity, it appears that house cats have lost about a third of their neurons.

The scientists then compared the brains from kittens of both species and made an interesting discovery. At birth, both have a full complement of retinal ganglion cells—roughly one million. But as adults, domestic cats lose all but 160,000 of them. While this may be all the cells needed to watch life from a windowsill, the discovery sheds light on the possible neural plasticity of felines. Should their environment change, domestic cats, at least, may have the neural potential to cope.

A North American lynx (*Lynx canadensis*) is momentarily airborn as it chases a rabbit. Although they feed almost exclusively on snowshoe hares, lynx occasionally kill deer and caribou fawns and scavenge from moose and deer carcasses.

2

The Big Cats

The eyes of the tiger are the brightest of any animal on earth. At dusk, or in the beam of a torch, they blaze back the ambient light with awe-inspiring intensity. It would be a tragedy . . . if we allowed that magical fire to burn out.

—ARJAN SINGH, *Tiger! Tiger!* 1984

The streamlined beauty and sleek, muscled definition of a large cat are captivating. Reminiscent of our small, devoted house cats, they look like bigger versions to pet and cuddle. Yet these spotted and bronzed felines are intelligent, agile meat-eaters that often view us more as potential prey than predatory equals. The big cats live in a sensory world alien to humans, one that has been perfected by evolution for the main purpose of detecting and subduing their next carnivorous meal.

The *Panthera*—lions, tigers, leopards, and jaguars—are called the *great cats*. Not only are they the largest of all felid species, but they are the only ones that can roar. Their loud vocalizations are made possible by the presence of an ossified hyoid bone in their voice box. The rest of the felid species lack such specialized vocal anatomy, including a few large cats, like the mountain lion, snow leopard, clouded leopard, and cheetah. In fact, the clouded leopard is often considered intermediary in size between the "big cats" and the many species of small felids.

Large cats have been described as the ultimate warriors—designed for stealth, power, and speed. Few animals can transform as quickly from cute to deadly. They are a mesmerizing combination of strength and grace—superior to us as athletes and our rivals in intelligence. So strong is the tiger that it can knock down prey two to three times heavier than itself.

"Big cats talk to each other along trails and roads through their scrapes and feces," explains felid specialist Alan Rabinowitz with the Wildlife Conservation Society (formerly the New York Zoological Society). "Each mark tells a different story, such as the sex and age of the animal and whether or not a female is in estrus." To defend territories, find mates, obtain food, and raise their young, cats communicate with each other by voice, facial expression, body language, and a range of chemical signals.

More than a quarter century ago, George Schaller warned that man and the big cats cannot coexist. "We have witnessed their demise over most of North America, Europe, South Asia, and North and South Africa," he said. "Wherever human populations have increased, the big cats have inevitably decreased."

Above: **The cougar or puma (*Felis concolor*) has the most extensive range of any land mammal in the Western Hemisphere, from the Canadian Yukon through the rain forests of South America to Patagonia.**

Opposite: **The royal head and classic mane of the male lion (*Panthera leo*) signal dominance and danger. Lions are the only felid species to show such obvious sexual dimorphism. The mane helps protect its owner during battles, and indicates his age, health, and status.**

According to UCLA physiologist Jared Diamond (*Natural History,* August 1992), "If keystone species are gone—those species of overwhelming importance to ecosystem function—then what we're trying to preserve is no longer the pristine self-sustaining ecosystem that nature could manage unassisted, but an already collapsing ecosystem incapable of sustaining itself." When major predators are eliminated, says Diamond, nonviable "rump communities" are created that require continuous human intervention.

"The reason I study big cats," concludes Rabinowitz, "is not that they are more special than other animals. They are important because they are large, solitary, secretive carnivores. They are environmental markers, and they are going the fastest. If we can save them, there is hope that we can save other wildlife. I am so grateful that I lived at a time when I could experience these big cats in the wild. If a time comes when we no longer value them, and they are gone, I hope that I am too."

THE LION

Panthera leo

In the dark all cats are gray, and these cats, big as they are, vanish like gray smoke after a few paces.

> —*MAITLAND EDEY, The Cats of Africa, 1968*

Renowned wildlife artist Robert Bateman painted an African scene with lions (*International Wildlife,* May/June 1983) in which one stands to the far right on a canvas dominated by habitat, and three others are lying on the ground to the far left. "This is the way you usually see lions," he explains, "for in fact you *don't* see them. You'll stop your car to look at one lion on the horizon, and when you start the car again, suddenly four or five other heads will appear from nowhere."

I once experienced this lion invisibility factor during a foot safari in Zambia's Luangwa Valley. Stepping in the dried footprints of elephants and antelope, we suddenly came upon a pride of lions resting around a termite mound. Our guide, carrying an antiquated elephant gun with two bullets, froze and gestured in earnest that we should back away quietly, or, more directly, get the hell out of there. The dry grass was high enough to conceal the big cats, and sure enough, not all of them were with the main group. The guide's fear of the cats, and of being encircled by them, remains with me to this day.

Now restricted to sub-Saharan Africa and to the protection of national parks and wildlife reserves in East Africa, African lions can be found

After lounging for hours during the day, lions become active at dusk, often roaming for miles in search of prey.

are left in the wild, and their numbers are continuing to decline. Most can be found in the reserves and parks in southern and eastern Africa, with a remnant population of Asiatic lions encapsulated in the Gir Forest of India. In areas where they are not hunted, such as Africa's national parks, lions are conspicuous, fearless animals, easily habituated to tourist vehicles. Where unprotected and threatened by people, lions become nearly invisible by staying quietly nocturnal.

ASIATIC LIONS

Panthera leo persica

At one time Asiatic lions ranged from eastern Europe, across the semidesert regions of Syria, Mesopotamia, and Persia, east to central India. The lions entered India from central Europe through the northwestern passes and spread over most of northern and central India. First eliminated from eastern Europe and Palestine, these regal cats survived until the early nineteenth century. Human expansion, coupled with the use of firearms, soon eliminated the rest. By 1884, only about a dozen remained. Eventually, the last intact population of Asiatic lions survived on private property in the Gir forest of Saurashtra in the hills of western India.

In 1890, the Newab rulers of Junagadh in India's Gujarat State declared the remaining lions protected and banned all hunting. In 1947, the same year that India gained its independence, the Gir Forest was declared a reserve. In 1965, it was designated a wildlife sanctuary. The Gir Lion Sanctuary Project was launched in 1975 and a one-meter-high rubble wall was erected around four hundred kilometers of the sanctuary to keep out cattle. It continues to be illegal to kill a lion in or outside of the sanctuary.

Similar in size to the African lions, the Asiatic subspecies averages about nine feet in length. They are more gray in coloration with longer tufts of hair at the elbows. A fringe-lined fold of skin along their bellies differentiates them from their African cousins.

Despite protection, India's prized Asiatic lions are under continued pressure. Sanctuary resources are shared with people and livestock as well as with other protected wildlife. Cattle grazing, grass cutting, cultivation, and timber harvesting are permitted within the sanctuary. Crops of cotton, wheat, millet, sugar cane, and groundnut grown on the fertile black soil surrounding the sanctuary have eliminated both cover and range for the lions and the wild and domestic herbivores they stalk.

The competition for resources is probably most apparent in the pirating of lion kills by local hide collectors. Gir lions feed almost exclusively on cattle. Sometimes, before they can feed on their kill, the lions are chased off the carcass by the impoverished Harijan people bordering the sanctuary, who then eat the meat and sell the hides. Because the Indian government compensates owners for cat-killed cattle, the lions have become middlemen in an unconventional welfare system in which people are compensated for stealing and eating the lions' food. More recently, due to a cattle-killing drought, the lions have taken to killing people encountered while jumping thorn enclosures and entering houses in search of livestock.

In 1980, I had a chance to visit this remote area of India located on the Kathiawar Peninsula in Gujarat state. Flying from Goa over the Gulf of Kutch in the Arabian Sea, we arrived in Keshod. An Indian driver and guide picked us up at the airport in a white car with spray-painted blue windows. En route to the Gir Forest, the betel-nut-chewing driver played chicken on the narrow road with each three-wheeled taxi, ox cart, and horn-honking truck we passed. Everywhere you looked there was life, and death. The trip took us past milling crowds of people, dogs, cows, pigs, sheep, hairy pigs, and water buffalo—all mixed together on the dusty streets. A truck ran into a horse cart, knocking the horse to the ground in the middle of the road. Nearby a dead pig, sprawled in the middle of town, was being eaten by crows. Women in gold-threaded saris carried huge loads of cut grass on their heads; others carried enormous brass pots that glistened in the sun.

It took two and a half hours to drive from Keshod to the Gir Forest Wildlife Sanctuary, which is inhabited as much by people and cattle as wildlife. It wasn't at all what I had expected. There were people everywhere leading goats and cattle home. The riverbed adjacent to the sanctuary was cultivated. As I talked to a ranger, I was served tea in a saucer. We did see lions that day, as part of a huge crowd of people who gathered for the afternoon "lion show." The lions lay in the nearby grass as the noisy crowd talked, smoked, and giggled less than fifty yards away.

Opposite: **Two lion cubs (*Panthera leo*) rest in a tree in Botswana's Okavango Delta.**

and tigers kill leopards, which weigh only one-fourth as much as they do. Although sympatric with tigers and lions over much of their range, leopards remain ecologically separated from both through direct avoidance and different habitat utilization. Ironically, the leopard's flexible behavior traits due to such subordination have helped make it more resilient to human intrusion and habitat disturbance. Willing to kill and eat just about any animal, leopards are faring slightly better than the lion and cheetah in Africa.

Once thought to be a separate species, all-black leopards, called panthers, are quite common. They have normal spots, but their background coat color is so dark that the spots can only be seen in direct sunlight. It is now known that all-black and spotted leopards can occur in the same litter.

Leopards use specific pathways while hunting within their home range and will habitually use the same tree in which to cache and eat their prey. They maintain their territories by scent marking, roaring, and conspicuous movement throughout their home range. Scent marking can include spraying urine, face-rubbing against objects, scraping, drooling, lying down, rolling on the ground, and scratching tree trunks. The most socially dominant cats mark most frequently. Both olfaction (glandular and urine) and audition play important but separate roles in leopard communication.

Female leopards reproduce slowly, producing two or three cubs once every couple of years. In areas with many competing predators, few cubs survive to adulthood. Photographer Art Wolfe discovered what one tree-climbing female did with her young cub. He watched a leopardess lying on a tree branch in Kenya's Samburu National Park, slowly get up, stretch, then climb down the trunk and past his vehicle to disappear in the bushes. Moments later, the leopardess reappeared with a young kitten that she had hidden on the ground.

Because ungulate density directly influences leopard density, field research has shown that the presence of reliable water sources positively influ-

Having dispatched a wild hare, a leopard rests for a moment, its beautiful spotted coat aglow in the South African sun. Extremely adaptable, leopards appear to be faring slightly better than lions and cheetahs as their habitat and prey are lost to human development.

ences the reproductive success of female leopards by helping to stabilize resident prey populations. This finding has important implications for the conservation of these and other large felines.

"Leopards are real opportunists and probably the most adaptable of the big cats," says Randy Eaton. "When crowded by man, they simply alter their habits by snatching up his dogs or goats, often becoming a nuisance." As a result, leopards have been eliminated as pests throughout most of northern and southern Africa. And they continue to be killed for their pelts. To denote prestige and power, leopard skins and claw necklaces are still worn today by African leaders such as the Zulu king and the head of the Inkatha Freedom Party in South Africa. Yet a pair of leopards will not produce enough cubs in a lifetime to make a single full-length coat.

Because leopards habitually use the same arboreal pathways and caches, they are easily baited, poisoned, and shot. Poaching and the indiscriminate use of heavy pesticides have affected the health of leopard populations, as has the crush of human population. Adequate cover in the form of shrubs and trees, for hunting and to cache kills, appears to be a limiting habitat factor for leopards. Charcoal burning, timber exploitation, and agricultural development have also accelerated the decline in the leopard population.

For example, the Amur leopard, native to the forested mountains of Russia's remote far east, is one of the most endangered cats in the world. Less than fifty are thought to survive in the wild. Named after the river that forms the border between Russia and China, the Amur leopard survives in a narrow mountain chain from Russia's Hanka Lake south to the borders of North Korea and China. The most northerly ranging of any leopard subspecies, its long winter coat with large spots gives it the appearance of a snow leopard.

What little is known about these leopards has come from painstaking studies in Kedrovaya Pad Nature Reserve near Vladivostok. With roe deer, its preferred prey, now scarce, Amur leopards are sometimes forced to make a single kill last for two weeks or more. In between, they scrounge for carrion when no deer or smaller prey is available. Severely threatened due to habitat loss, loss of prey, and human persecution, the Amur leopard's snowy footprints across fallen logs and rock ledges may soon mark yet another poignant path to extinction.

CHEETAH

Acinonyx jubatus

Cheetahs are so noticeably different from other members of the *Felidae,* with a few features unlike any other cat, that they have been given their own genus. To begin with, these slender, graceful, high-speed cats are the world's fastest terrestrial mammals. Relying on speed to survive, they can run nearly 70 miles per hour over short distances—accelerating from 0 to 45 mph in just two seconds. Covering twenty feet in a stride, they zigzag after a fleeing gazelle with the agility of a skilled slalom racer.

Not as powerful as the other big cats, cheetahs have the regal, aristocratic look of a thorough-bred. A black line running from each eye to the corner of the mouth accentuates the cat's eyes, giving it a designer appearance. These tear lines probably serve the same purpose as a football player's black face grease—to help reduce the sun's glare. Most important, the dramatic facial markings help facilitate visual communication between these fleet-footed, day-active cats.

Standing thirty inches high at the shoulders, with the slim, streamlined build of a runner, cheetahs are definitely the greyhounds of the feline family. Like greyhounds, they, too, have small heads, a broad, muscular chest, and an elongated torso for running. Built lean, slightly swaybacked, with a flexible spine and long legs for maximum stride, cheetahs use their long tails for counterbalance. Their large nasal passages and lungs help supply the oxygen needed during their high-performance runs and facilitate post-sprint cooling. Like all cats, cheetahs run on their toes, but their blunt exposed claws seem more canid than cat. Another adaptation for the chase, their protruding claws and hard footpads provide greater traction while running.

Cheetahs were once widely distributed throughout Africa and southwest Asia. Today these endangered felines are restricted to the remaining grasslands and open woodlands found south of the Sahara. Nearly extinct, an isolated

Opposite: A recessive gene causes some leopards to have black fur. Called black panthers, these melanistic leopards are just as spotted as their normal littermates, but the characteristic markings can be seen only in bright light.

Below: A South African leopard demonstrates how effective its cryptic coloration is for conceal-ment. Unfortunately, human fashion also favors spots, and leop-ards, like many of the exotically marked felines, fall prey to poachers.

population of two hundred Asian cheetahs (*A. jubatus venaticus*) survive in Iran and possibly a few still inhabit northwest Afghanistan. Otherwise, *A. jubatus* is the last of four cheetah species that once stalked North America and the Old World two million to ten thousand years ago.

The cheetah's regal beauty, intelligence, and mild manner, coupled with its ability to hunt at greyhound speeds, has made this cat a coveted pet and hunting companion among nobility throughout history. Sumerians and Egyptian pharaohs trained them to course after prey. According to Marco Polo, Kublai Khan kept a thousand cheetahs for summer hunts in Mongolia—dressing them in close-fitting leather caps. The Mogul emperor Akbar the Great reportedly kept nine thousand Asian cheetahs during his reign. At one time or another, rulers of Russia, India, France, Austria, and Arabia have all used cheetahs in hunts. Charlemagne, Genghis Khan, and Haile Selassie of Ethiopia all kept cheetahs as pets.

Cheetahs are shy felines, yet their day-active behavior makes them the most conspicuous of Africa's predators. Sunlight better illuminates their high-speed chases. It also keeps most nocturnal carnivores at bay, giving cheetahs a chance to hunt and eat in peace. Even so, their highly visible chases often attract other predators eager to steal the warm carcass. Cheetahs are unable to compete against lions, leopards, and hyenas. To avoid debilitating injuries that could lead to starvation, they simply abandon their kills during confrontations with these predators. This loss of food, hunting time, and energy puts cheetahs at further risk in stressed environments. Unlike other felid species, cheetahs do not scavenge or cache their food.

Cheetahs hunt by sight, sometimes using termite mounds as lookout posts. The majority of their diet consists of impalas, gazelles, and other small antelopes, but they also kill ostriches, birds, hares, and lizards. Once prey is targeted, the cheetah advances like an invisible air current, moving forward each time the antelope grazes, freezing the second it looks up. When just fifty to one hundred yards away, the cheetah explodes from cover in an effort to cuff and topple the prey. Moving like a spring coil, long tail circling for balance, swivel hips making quick high-speed turns, a racing cheetah is a sight to behold. At times, all four feet lift off the ground simultaneously. Should the cat succeed in tripping the

antelope, it quickly secures a stranglehold that cuts off air—and life—within minutes.

Following such a high-speed chase, cheetahs usually need time to recover before eating, yet it is in their best interest to feed quickly, before their kill is detected by the intimidating gang of four—leopards, lions, hyenas, and vultures. Cheetahs lose about 10 percent of their hard-earned kills to these persistent predators. Both lions and leopards readily attack and kill cheetahs given the opportunity. Tourist vehicles can also interfere with cheetah hunts. When congregated around a pile of photogenic cheetah cubs, the vehicles sometimes attract predators that then add to the photo op moment by killing and eating the cubs.

But not always. When a warthog fatally pierced the lung of a female cheetah with five cubs in Kenya's Masai Mara, tour drivers who witnessed the event provisioned the orphaned young with meat. Despite a high density of lions in the area, the cubs were old enough to survive without their mother. Habituated to people, the full-grown cubs now sit on the hoods of tourist vehicles, their tails flipped nonchalantly over windshields.

Cheetahs normally travel alone, in pairs, or in small groups of related kin—such as a family of cubs that have not yet left home. A pile of resting cheetahs becomes an optical illusion of shape and form concealed by spots, an artistic rendering of congenial family life. Mutual grooming reinforces the social bonds among wild cheetahs. Sitting and lying as a group in star formation, heads toward the center, they simultaneously lick each other's faces. Females typically initiate grooming with older, larger males. It is while grooming that cheetahs purr the loudest.

Three to six cheetah cubs are born following a ninety-day gestation period. Although camouflaged in natal coats that seem to mimic the shaggy hyena look, many cubs die during their first two months of life because the female is unable to defend them against rival predators. While still young, the cubs remain hidden when their mother goes to hunt. However, their habit of scattering when startled can be a liability when flushed by a pride of lions or pack of hyenas. As an antipredator strategy, females move their cubs from lair to lair, up to fifteen to twenty times, during the cubs' first weeks of life. Even so, cub mortality often runs as high as 70 percent.

Cheetah moms call their cubs with a throaty

Opposite: With an air of regal elegance, a cheetah (*Acinonyx jubatus*) sits poised in the Kenya bush. From Egypt to India, cheetahs were once trained to hunt game on command in an exotic sport called coursing.

In a blur of spots, a cheetah (*Acinonyx jubatus*) flies over the ground in pursuit of an impala. The cheetah uses its tail like a rudder to help make quick direction changes while chasing such fast prey.

staccato purr. The young answer with birdlike chirps. When three months old, the cubs follow the female during hunts. Her characteristic chirruping call summons the cubs to feed on a fresh kill. Once full, the cubs curl up around their mother and purr loudly.

Cheetah moms have their work cut out for them. Not only do they feed their cubs from birth to six months of age by themselves, but they spend considerable time and energy teaching the cubs how to hunt when they are six to twelve months old—while still providing most of their food. Once the cubs become efficient predators, at about a year old, they all hunt together.

The cubs separate from their mother at fourteen to eighteen months of age. To withstand harassment from spotted hyenas and rival male cheetahs, the cubs remain together for another six months. At that time, the females gradually split away to establish overlapping ranges with their mother. Meanwhile, the young males are forced by mature, breeding males to migrate great distances from their natal range—often outside park boundaries. To better compete, male siblings often form all-male coalitions that may eventually include an unrelated male. Such coalitions last the cheetah's lifetime.

Like all felines, cheetahs rely on a system of olfactory communication. To scent-mark their

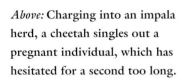

Above: Charging into an impala herd, a cheetah singles out a pregnant individual, which has hesitated for a second too long.

Right: Cheetahs kill their prey by first knocking it to the ground to get a strangulation hold on the throat.

home ranges, male cheetahs leave urine messages on tree trunks, rocks, termite mounds, and other noticeable objects. During the tail-up delivery of the odoriferous liquid, males tread or "skate" with their hind feet. Prior to marking an object, the cheetah touches it with the tip of its tail and continues to move its tail over the object once squirting begins. Tactile information provided by the tail apparently helps direct the stream of urine.

As endearing as these traits may be, cheetahs are in trouble. As few as ten thousand survive in the wild. Listed as endangered throughout their remaining range, these aristocratic cats are losing turf. Due to their prey requirements and hunting technique, cheetahs are restricted to open grasslands, but such habitat covers only about 5 percent of Africa south of the Sahara. Not only do cheetahs depend on specific types of habitat, but on certain types and size of prey. As a result, cheetahs often require a much larger range area to survive than do the tiger or leopard. In the Serengeti, where 90 percent of the female cheetah's diet consists of Thomson's gazelle, their annual home range can encompass three hundred square miles, the acreage needed to follow the migratory routes of the antelope.

Because much of their open habitat is now being used for subsistence agriculture and livestock, cheetahs are endangered due to habitat loss and starvation, as well as drought and poaching. In Namibia, farmers kill hundreds of cheetahs each year. Adding to their woes are domestic cats that have infected cheetahs in Serengeti National Park with feline immunodeficiency virus (FIV). A high cub mortality rate is also contributing to the species' decline.

In Asia, the cheetah is nearly extinct. The last three cheetahs in India were killed in 1951. Conservation efforts in Iran are the last hope for the Asian cheetah, where the few that remain are well protected in wildlife reserves. In Africa, cheetah populations continue to decline. The species is extinct in much of north and west Africa, where healthy populations once existed. Cheetahs are also shot for their beautiful spotted skins. Unrestricted hunting and the illegal trade in skins have decimated cheetahs in Ethiopia and Somalia.

Cheetahs in captivity have also had problems. Captive records indicate that, since 1956 when the Philadelphia Zoo was the first twentieth-century facility to produce cheetahs in captivity, less

Four near-grown littermates rest in a close tactile pile in Kenya's Masai Mara. Provisioned by tour drivers after their mother was killed by a warthog, these cheetahs have been habituated to people.

than 15 percent of wild-caught cheetahs have bred in zoos, fewer than 25 percent of captive adults breed more than once, and nearly 40 percent of the cubs born in captivity die soon after birth. By looking at the cheetahs' reproductive physiology and molecular genetics, scientists discovered part of the reason why.

Roughly ten thousand years ago a genetic bottleneck occurred when more than 99 percent of all cheetahs were wiped out in the wild. The few that survived provided the limited genetic stock for all future generations. As a result, modern cheetahs are as genetically identical as highly inbred lab mice—cats from distinct geographic areas appear as if genetically cloned. This situation has weakened their immune system and helped jeopardize their reproduction. Inbreeding has led to male sperm counts that are 90 percent lower than tigers' and lions'. Moreover, roughly 75 percent of the cheetah sperm that is produced is abnormal. In the livestock trade, males with an abnormal sperm count of just 20 percent would be tossed out as infertile.

While much recent emphasis has been given to molecular genetics to explain the cheetah's infertility problems, other scientists are looking at zoo management issues to identify possible behavioral elements. Captive management policies are being reviewed in terms of enclosure size, the ability of males to compete for breeding rights, and the chance for a female to choose her mate.

The three-thousand-acre Fossil Rim Wildlife Center, located 75 miles southwest of Dallas, has had extraordinary success at breeding cheetahs. Five cats brought to the Center in 1986 turned into fifty-five in just six years. Many are now on "breeding loans" to other facilities.

To help increase cheetah fertility in zoos, the olfactory skills of male cheetahs are now being enlisted. Three times a week, males are brought into the females' enclosures after the females have been removed. When a female is in estrus, the male begins to stutter bark, a behavioral response to the strong olfactory message that a female is in heat. Zoo staff then make sure the female has a chance to mate.

Both in distribution and density, the cheetah has never been as successful as the leopard. Throughout their range, cheetah numbers are declining. In 1980, there were an estimated six thousand cheetahs in Namibia in southwestern Africa. By 1991 only about twenty-five hundred remained. Because cheetahs follow Thomson's and Grant's gazelles in their seasonal migrations

Following a ninety- to ninety-five-day gestation period, up to six cheetah cubs are born in a den hidden in tall vegetation. At birth, the cubs are camouflaged in a distinctive natal coat that is light gray on top with a black belly. A woolly, hyena-like ridge of fur runs down their necks and backs.

A cheetah and her kitten relax in the fading light of Kenya's Masai Mara Game Reserve.

Recorded sightings of the striped, or king, cheetah were rare and only a few skins existed. It wasn't until nearly fifty years later, in 1974, that the first photograph of the cat was finally taken in South Africa's Kruger National Park.

Initially, the king cheetah was described as a leopard-cheetah hybrid and classified as a new species. In fact, hair samples analyzed at the Institute of Medical Research in Johannesburg revealed that the king's cuticular scale pattern more closely resembled that of a leopard than the common cheetah.

Captive reproduction and molecular genetics helped settle the debate. The distinctive king coat pattern is the result of a mutation inherited as a single autosomal recessive allele. Most felids are marked with spots, rosettes, or stripes over an agouti background. Domestic cat breeders discovered that a striped tabby could produce kittens with blotched markings not unlike the markings on a king cheetah. This mutant pattern is apparently controlled by a single locus, appropriately called the "tabby locus." The king blotches probably result from a mutation at the same locus. In captivity, king cheetahs of both sexes have been produced from normally marked, or wild type, cheetahs and from their offspring.

TIGER

Panthera tigris

The Indian tiger is a creature of hypnotic power and fascination. The more one sees of this beautiful beast, the more one is charmed by its gorgeous color, the vivid pattern of the stripes on its glossy skin, the strength of the muscles and the grace of the tiger's movements. But the tiger is far from being just a beautiful big cat. It is at the apex of nature's pyramid, a balancing force on all the animals and creatures within its kingdom.

—*KAILASH SANKHALA*

in search of forage, few parks are big enough to contain these felid thoroughbreds of the African plains. According to Norman Myers, only an ecosystem approach to saving a species will help this cat survive into the twenty-first century.

KING CHEETAHS: SOUTH AFRICA

In 1926, a strange-looking cat with distinctive black dorsal stripes and black blotches instead of spots was reportedly sighted in Zimbabwe. At first, everyone thought a new species of cheetah had been discovered and debate ensued.

BENGAL TIGER

Panthera tigris tigris

The tiger is the largest member of the cat family. A full-grown tiger is roughly fifty times heavier than a domestic cat and, when stretched out, can be longer than a horse. It has been described as a mobile battering ram, able to knock down animals weighing more than twice its own weight. The strongest and most dangerous of all cats, the tiger is an impressive feline. It has the largest canine teeth of any terrestrial carnivore. The Siberian tiger, the biggest of eight tiger subspecies, can weigh nearly eight hundred pounds, and measure an impressive thirteen feet from nose to tail tip. Its tail can be as long as its body.

The Indian or Bengal tiger is a formidable, five-hundred-pound predator. Not surprisingly, it is the national animal of India. Native to temperate and tropical Asia, these dramatic felines inhabit the forests and mangrove swamps of India, Burma, Bangladesh, Bhutan, and Nepal. In addition to their size, strength, and reputation as *carnivore extraordinaire*, tigers hold title as the only cat with a black-striped orange coat.

This distinctive coat color seems flamboyant for a large cat, but, in fact, it helps its owner disappear among patches of shadow and light in the forests and grasslands. Like a mirage, the stripes break up the outline of the tiger's body, enabling the cat to hide and make silent, secretive approaches toward its prey. The pattern of stripes is unique to each animal. Face markings are so distinctive as to be used for identification.

Equipped with sharp, retractable claws, long canines, and muscular forelegs, tigers stalk and ambush their prey from about thirty feet, charging from the side or behind to deliver a quick, lethal bite to the back of the neck or the throat. These efficient, solitary hunters can eat up to eighty pounds of meat in a night, dining on sambar deer, gaur, buffalo, wild pigs, and small mammals, birds, and fish. "The forest goes dead silent when a tiger is nearby," says Alan Rabinowitz. "The birds, insects, everything becomes deadly quiet."

The beautiful king, or striped, cheetah (*Acinonyx jubatus*) is not a separate species, but the result of a rare genetic mutation. King cheetah cubs can be born among normally marked littermates.

Tigers stalk and kill animals as large as young elephants, rhinos, and bears, but as opportunistic carnivores, they will also catch smaller fare such as rodents, crabs, and frogs. Indian wildlife photographer Rajesh Bedi once photographed a tigress feeding on a freshly killed leopard. Where their natural food supply has been reduced due to habitat loss and competition from human hunters, tigers frequently resort to killing livestock and, occasionally, people.

Excellent swimmers, tigers are probably the most water-loving of felines. Intolerant of the sun and heat, they can often be found cooling off in pools or streams on hot, humid days, or sleeping in the coolest part of the forest.

Tigers will freely enter rivers and streams to chase prey. As solitary hunters, tigers have to outsmart their prey. They have been observed hiding beside a river or pond, waiting for prey to come and drink. The tiger then singles out and chases an animal into deep water where it holds its victim underwater until it drowns.

Tigers live up to their reputation as the largest felines. The average male Bengal tiger measures ten feet from nose to tail, stands thirty-six inches high at the shoulder, and carries a massive head that is sixteen inches long by ten inches wide. Usually a full-grown tiger weighs between 400 and 500 pounds. The female is generally about a foot shorter and 100 pounds lighter than the male. The male patrols and scent-marks his territory to warn off potential intruders, spraying urine on objects at tiger nose level.

Solitary and secretive, tigers are extremely difficult to observe in the wild. In an area free of humans, they are usually active at dawn and dusk. The tiger's bold double stripes, which appear so conspicuous in captivity, provide ideal camouflage in reeds, elephant grass, or a twilight forest. "Even when he is sitting cooling himself in water," explains Sankhala, "the dazzling sun confuses the eye and a tiger can easily be taken for a river boulder."

"The tiger is a first-class naturalist," wrote Charles McDougal in The Face of the Tiger (1977), "and knows the seasonal and daily activity patterns of the various prey animals—where they may be found, and when they will be feeding or resting. When hunting, the tiger moves slowly, making maximum use of cover for concealment, frequently pausing to listen and watch. The tiger depends on its eyes and ears to locate prey."

Throughout the tiger's range in Asia, two prey types predominate: wild pigs and large deer. The major prey of the Bengal tiger are chital (spotted deer), sambar (a large Asiatic deer), and wild pigs. Tigers may roam considerable distances in a day in search of food. They typically stalk and ambush their prey, charging their victim from relatively short distances. The prey is killed in thirty-five to ninety seconds by a bite to the nape of the neck or by a suffocating throat hold.

After making the kill, the tiger usually drags the carcass into seclusion to feed. It has been said that a tiger has the traction power of thirty men; it is capable of hauling off an animal as large as a buffalo or a young rhino weighing up to one thousand pounds. A tiger will feed on a large kill for three or four days. Tigers are notoriously neat feeders, and their fastidiousness makes it possible to distinguish a tiger kill from that of any other predator.

The pads of the tiger's feet are soft and particularly sensitive to heat, and they restrict its pursuit of prey through prickly undergrowth or rough terrain. The tiger's heavy build limits an attack to one or two powerful springs, after which surviving prey may easily escape. Although there is an advantage to hunting solo in dense vegetation, the tiger's solitary lifestyle can be fatal if the animal is injured or unable to hunt.

During field research in India's Kanha National Park, George Schaller (The Deer and the Tiger, 1967) observed that tigers make an average of nineteen unsuccessful stalks for every kill. Maintaining a feast-or-famine regime, the tiger gorges itself when it does finally eat. Schaller estimated that a tiger needs twelve to fifteen pounds of meat a day. He then figured that if a tiger eats only 70 percent of a given carcass with minimal disturbance, then it must kill 6,300 to 7,800 pounds of prey per year.

Once detected, the tiger's presence is advertised by alarm calls of deer, monkeys, agitated peafowl, junglefowl, and a variety of other birds. The warning calls of barking deer and the "ponking" call of the sambar deer, indicating that a tiger is on the move, are among the more familiar sounds of the Indian jungle. Tigers must rotate hunting areas once prey species become aware of their presence.

Tigers breed throughout the year, with a major peak from November to April. Ovulation

Opposite: Tigers (*Panthera tigris*) lead a life of feast or famine, preying on deer, wild pigs, and smaller animals, such as monkeys, rodents, and reptiles. After subduing large prey, they usually drag it into seclusion, where they will feed on it for several days.

is induced by mating, which can be a noisy affair. "Conceive a chorus got up by a hundred pairs of cats," suggested E. Baker in 1887, "multiply copiously, and even then you will fail to realize the awful sounds." Legends from Manchuria tell of men tied to trees as a form of punishment when the December nights were filled with the nerve-shattering roars of mating tigers.

A short gestation of fifteen to sixteen weeks concludes with the birth of cubs weighing only two and a half to four pounds. The normal litter size is two to three cubs, but up to seven unborn fetuses have been removed from a pregnant tigress shot by hunters. Cubs are dependent on the female for one and a half to two years, after which they disperse with a 50 percent chance of survival.

According to Schaller, "If a tigress in the wild produces her first litter at the age of four and raises just one cub per year until she dies at the age of eighteen, her total lifetime production would be about fourteen animals. Under the conditions existing in India today, a tigress that raises even half that number before her death is doing better than average."

Most tigers die as a result of their inexperience in hunting or through encounters with humans. It is the young tiger, newly on its own, that runs the greatest risk. Cubs are killed in brush fires, preyed upon by jackals, killed in hunting accidents, disabled and starved after encounters with porcupines, and killed by male tigers. Adult tigers are occasionally disemboweled by rogue boars. Crocodiles have attacked and killed tigers in the water. A wild ox or buffalo may gore a tiger; a pack of Indian wild dogs, or dholes, easily scare a tiger. Schaller points out that in India more adult tigers die as a result of having been shot, speared, snared, or poisoned by man than through any other, natural cause.

Since the turn of the century, much of the tiger's natural prey has vanished due to human activities. Forest animals have been replaced by domestic livestock, forcing these large cats to occasionally prey on cattle. The Indian tiger was not listed as an endangered species until 1969. In 1972, a census organized by the Indian government concluded that only 1,827 tigers remained in India, with about 150 in Nepal, 180 in Bhutan, and 100 in Bangladesh. During the same year the World Wildlife Fund

(WWF) launched Operation Tiger, an international program aimed mainly at preserving the Bengal tiger.

After more than twenty years of effort to save India's tigers in protected reserves, biologists believe that less than 3,000 Bengal tigers may remain, a figure that could still doom the subspecies to extinction. In 1993, during former Pakistani Prime Minister Nawaz Sharif's re-election campaign, he chose the tiger as his

election symbol. Yet due to the lack of available tigers, stand-in lions had to be hired as his traveling mascots instead.

Three of the eight subspecies of tigers have already gone extinct. If the remaining five, including the Bengal tiger, are to survive, large tracts of land must be preserved in order to support their plant-eating prey, home ranges, and the need for subadults to disperse long distances. Ultimately, the tiger's survival will depend on developing creative ways for people and tigers to use the same space.

Central to Indian life is a religious, mystical bond between man and nature. At the turn of the century, an estimated forty to fifty thousand tigers roamed the forests of India. The subcontinent was teeming with wildlife—350 species of mammals and 1,200 species of birds. Much of it was paraded past guests on royal estates as a show of wealth and hospitality. Maharajas held

Creating an optical illusion with its vertical orange coat and black stripes, a Bengal tiger (*Panthera tigris tigris*) weighing up to five hundred pounds can become nearly invisible against the dry grass of India.

Tigers are endangered throughout their natural range. Three subspecies, including the Javan, Caspian, and Bali tigers, have all gone extinct since the 1940s.

annual wildlife shoots and competed with each other to see who could kill the most animals, tigers in particular. High marks went to the Maharaja of Surguja who claimed he killed 1,150 tigers. Ironically, it was in those very forest pockets that had once been the exclusive game preserves of the Indian princes that the remaining tigers survived.

In an effort to save the tigers and preserve what was left of their complex ecosystem, the government of India and the World Wildlife Fund converted several of the former royal preserves into nineteen tiger sanctuaries. During the 1970s and 1980s, it appeared that the recovering tiger population had more than doubled due to this conservation effort. However, recent tiger counts reveal that such figures may have been inflated and that Project Tiger is, in fact, in trouble. The reason? More than 850 million people and more than 2 billion head of cattle

deadly price tag on every tiger's head, making them more valuable dead than alive. Tiger wine, guaranteed to impart strength and virility to all who imbibe, has created an insatiable demand for tiger bones. Once again tigers are quietly disappearing—this time pulverized into an untraceable powder.

WHITE TIGERS

More than forty years have passed since Maharaja Shri Martand Singh found a white tiger cub with chocolate stripes and blue eyes whose mother had been killed. Although there had been earlier reports of white tigers in the jungles of India, this was the first white tiger ever captured in the wild. Unlike the common black leopards, white tigers are extremely rare in the wild. In hopes of producing more white tigers in captivity, the prince brought the cub to his palace and named it Mohan.

Mohan subsequently became quite famous. As an adult, he was mated with an orange tigress named Begum. They produced three litters of orange cubs. Only when Mohan was bred with a daughter from the second litter were four white cubs finally produced.

Today, white tigers can be found in zoos across the United States, Europe, and Asia as the result of intensive selective breeding. They are a living legacy to Mohan—the rare white tiger cub orphaned in the wild many years ago.

SIBERIAN TIGER

Panthera tigris altaica

The largest of all cats, the endangered Siberian tiger can weigh up to eight hundred pounds. Only about two hundred of these rare cats are

now compete with the native wildlife. In 1992, like an unexpected tsunami, sixty villagers stormed India's Ranthambhor National Park, beating up some unarmed forest officers in an attempt to seize park land for cultivation. At other parks, tigers have been mysteriously "committing suicide."

Such growing competiton for the striped cat's last habitat is just one problem. A burgeoning black market for medicinal products has put a

SUBSPECIES	POPULATION
Indo-Chinese tiger	Less than 1,200
Indian or Bengal tiger	Approximately 3,000
Siberian or Amur tiger	Less than 1,000
South China tiger	Less than 50
Sumatran tiger	Less than 400
Javan tiger	Extinct in the 1980s
Caspian tiger	Extinct in the 1970s
Bali tiger	Extinct in the 1940s

SOURCE:
The International Tiger Conservation Project sponsored by NYZS/The Wildlife Conservation Society

thought to survive in the wild; another eight hundred live in captivity. In 1992, fifty Siberian tigers were poached in Russia, roughly 15 to 25 percent of the total remaining population in the wild. Included was Lena, a female tiger radio-collared by feline specialist Maurice Hornocker, codirector of an American-Russian research team studying tiger feeding behavior and territory size in the Sikhote-Alin Biosphere Reserve outside Plastun. Buried under snow, her collar ended up signaling the site of her demise—and the location of her four orphaned cubs.

Before the fall of the Russian state, tigers were well protected by the authoritarian regime of communism. Closed borders, gun control, close supervision of foreigners, and strict conservation laws kept poachers at bay. Now the situation has changed. Ironically, democracy may have quickened the pace to extinction by putting a free market price tag on Russia's most endangered wildlife. With poaching laws now widely unenforced due to the country's more pressing social problems, traders have invaded the Soviet woods to harvest everything from pine nuts and ginseng to musk deer and tiger.

The incentives to kill are high. For $4,000 to $10,000 you can buy a Siberian tiger. The wildlife trader may even throw in the bones to sweeten the deal—or charge $100 a pound. With prices that high, and borders now open to markets in China, North Korea, and Taiwan, an impoverished Russian can easily live off a single tiger kill for five to ten years. Some traders promise they can produce four tigers within a day.

When not shot outright, Siberian tigers are losing turf to an invasion of Russian and multinational companies that are eager to exploit the untapped riches of the taiga. Korea's Hyundai Corporation has contracted to log 200,000 hectares, including an entire watershed. Stretching from the Ural Mountains to the Pacific, Siberia's taiga of pine, fir, spruce, and larch is a forest as large as the continental United States. It not only contains one-fourth of the world's timber reserves, but stores 40 million tons of carbon dioxide. It is estimated that 10 million acres are now being cleared each year as Russia sells enormous tracts of forest to foreign investors at one-twentieth of the world market price.

According to David Gordon, project coordinator for the Siberian Forest Protection Project, developed by the Pacific Energy and Resources Center in Sausalito, California, most carbon responsible for global warming is stored in soils, not trees. Clear-cutting will cause soil erosion, flooding, and silting problems—not to mention loss of tiger territory—destroying soils and releasing carbon.

In 1986, a Siberian tiger was caught prowling the streets of Vladivostok, the largest city in eastern Russia. Habitat loss has not only eliminated their large hunting territories, but also the natural prey base of wild boar and deer upon which they feed. As in other places where large cats are being squeezed by human development, hungry Siberian tigers lacking home turf and natural prey are forced to seek domestic substitutes. The Soviet press has reported other incidents where

Leucism, the lack of dark pigmentation, is best illustrated by the white lions of Timbavati and this captive white tiger from South Africa. First bred in India, white tigers are now selectively bred in zoos around the world.

tigers have invaded small towns to attack live-stock, dogs, and people. When forced into such direct contact with humans, the outcome never favors the big cats.

As an indicator species marking the overall health of its environment, the Siberian tiger, like all large cats, serves as a sentinel guarding the well-being and mysterious forces of Mother Nature. As each of these sentinels, standing at the apex of intricate food chains, falls to the ravaging economic demands of human population growth, we are hastening our rush to that moment of searing enlightenment, that moment when we will at last understand the essence of life's interconnectedness, only to have destroyed it.

JAVAN TIGER

Panthera tigris sondaica

For many years an estimated five tigers remained at the eastern end of the island of Java. Since 1980, there has been no sign of this endangered subspecies. Because Java is such a densely populated, highly deforested island, there was little hope that this subspecies could be saved and, apparently, it wasn't. Efforts to capture the last animals and bring them into the safety of captivity came too late.

SNOW LEOPARD

Panthera uncia

In the high mountains of Central Asia, at elevations approaching twenty thousand feet, lives the snow leopard, a phantom cat that is as beautiful as it is elusive. Found in the alpine and subalpine zones of India, Pakistan, Afghanistan, China, Nepal, Mongolia, Bhutan, and the former USSR from the Altai Mountains to the Hindu Kush to the Himalayas, the snow leopard, or ounce, is one of the least known of the big cats. Cryptically colored to blend into snow and rock, this resident of the remote "roof of the world" is shrouded both in mystery and myth.

"In the snow leopard," says expert Helen

Above: In the high mountains of central Asia, at elevations up to 18,400 feet, lives the snow leopard (*Panthera uncia*), a phantom cat that is as beautiful as it is elusive.

Overleaf: With a thick fur coat cryptically colored to blend into snow and rock, large forepaws that act like snowshoes, short fore-limbs, strong chest muscles, and a three-foot tail, snow leopards are well adapted for life in the high, rugged mountains.

Freeman, founder of Seattle's International Snow Leopard Trust, "we can feel the spirit of mountains. In this cat there is a freedom that few people will ever have—a freedom to roam a region so rugged and wild that it often defies you to put one foot in front of the other, let alone leap. And the animal lives there, not with destruction, but with beauty."

Rarely seen, the snow leopard was first photographed in the wild by zoologist George Schaller in 1970. During the 1980s, Rodney Jackson and Darla Hillard successfully tracked five snow leopards from a study site at Langu Gorge in the Himalaya of western Nepal. "The back-breaking terrain, basic diet of rice and potatoes, and lack of contact with the outside world were a small price to pay for the privilege of studying the exquisite snow leopard," explained Jackson (*Animal Kingdom,* July/August 1987). "Yet, in some respects it was like studying a ghost."

During their four-year study, they only saw the camouflaged felines eighteen times. Difficult field conditions combined with the cat's low numbers, sparse distribution, and secretive habits continue to hamper attempts to study snow leopards in the wild. No other feline lives at such high elevations. These cloud- and snow-colored cats are most active in the otherworld twilight of sunrise and sunset.

Snow leopards prefer steep terrain, especially cliffs from which they can spot prey. Superbly adapted to a high-altitude life in the cold, snow leopards have long, thick fur and wide, well-cushioned furry paws that can grip steep cliffs and snowshoe over soft snow. Short, powerful forelimbs, strong chest muscles for climbing, and a three-foot-long tail used for balancing make this feline an agile rock climber for stealthy pursuit of blue sheep, ibex, musk deer, tahr, wild boar, and marmot. Their spotted coats are as unique in pattern to each snow leopard as fingerprints are to people.

Called *sabu* by Tibetan villagers, the snow leopard is slightly smaller in size than the common leopard and has fewer spots, which are arranged in distinct rows. Including the long tail, an adult can reach seven feet in length and weigh 60 to 165 pounds. Unlike tigers, lions, leopards, and jaguars, snow leopards do not roar. Instead, they make a high-pitched yowl as they scrape and scent-spray their travel routes along streambeds and ridge lines.

Since the Central Asian highlands are inhabited by few large animals, prey species are not abundant. Like other big cats, the snow leopard must range widely in order to find adequate food. Radio telemetry has revealed that snow leopards move along the base or crests of cliffs, along river bluffs, and up or down ridges, ravines, and stream canyons, following the seasonal migration of their prey to different altitudes. Where native ungulates have been depleted, snow leopards have turned to domestic sheep and goats.

Today the shy, solitary snow leopard is endangered throughout its range due to prey and habitat loss and, consequently, to its elimination as a livestock pest. Even in the most remote areas, much of its habitat is now being utilized for livestock grazing, subsistence farming, or firewood collection. The continued black market demand for its luxurious spotted fur has also put this feline at risk. The cats are killed with poison-tipped spears angled along their trails.

As few as four thousand snow leopards may survive in the wild. Since 1981 the International Snow Leopard Trust has helped save these endangered cats through research, public education, and the establishment of a cooperative international conservation effort among twelve countries.

"The beauty and genius of a work of art may be reconceived, though its first material expression be destroyed—a vanished harmony may yet again inspire the composer," wrote American naturalist William Beebe. "But when the last individual of a race of living things breathes no more, another heaven and another earth must pass before such a one can be again." And so it is with the snow leopard.

JAGUAR

Panthera onca

The largest feline in the Western Hemisphere, the jaguar once roamed the swamps, jungles, and wooded regions of Arizona and New Mexico south to central Patagonia. However, *el tigre Americano,* like many wild felines, is now endangered throughout its range. The last documented report of a jaguar shot in the United States occurred in Cochise County, Arizona, in the late 1980s. Virtually extinct in its northern range, they now survive only in the most remote areas

from Mexico and Central America into South America, with the largest remaining population found in the Amazon rain forest.

Considered a New World equivalent to the tiger, jaguars are, in fact, the only "great cat" to be found in the Americas. Smaller than lions and tigers, but larger, more powerful, and more heavily built than leopards, jaguars are equipped with teeth and jaw musculature so developed that their bite is considered the most powerful of any of the big cats, relative to their size. Their all-meat diet includes armadillo, peccary, deer, paca, tapir, turtles, capybara, fish, and caiman. They also prey on arboreal monkeys such as howlers, which, like all prey, they bite through the head. A jaguar can crack a capybara's skull like a nut, using its canines to pop the skull bones out of their suture lines, crushing the brain in between. They are able to kill other animals, including cattle, in similar skull-bite style.

Jaguars are good tree climbers and swimmers. They attack prey in the water and use their front paws to flip fish onto streambanks. Jaguars silently patrol riverbanks and dense rain forest in search of prey. By culling deer, peccaries, and other highly productive mammals jaguars maintain prey species at habitat-carrying capacity. As scavengers, they eat dead fish and caiman carcasses left after floods and eliminate the decaying remains of large mammals.

The third largest feline in the world after tigers and lions, the jaguar is the largest and strongest cat native to the Americas. Giant jaguars as big as the ancient European cave lions once roamed throughout North America. Today, males weigh 120 to 250 pounds or more and reach lengths of seven feet including tail. The largest jaguars inhabit the Mato Grosso area of southwestern Brazil and northern Argentina.

Jaguars are more heavily built and muscled than a leopard, with thick legs, barrel chest, and a wider face than a leopard. Otherwise, both species are very much alike in coloration, niche preference, strength, and adaptability. Equally spotted with rosettes, the jaguar pelt can be differentiated from a leopard's by the one or more extra spots within the center of each circle. Albino jaguars have been sighted in Paraguay. Like leopards, jaguars also occur in a jet black melanistic phase. The color of night and daytime shadows, these nocturnal black cats are nearly invisible.

Indians from Mexico into South America revered the jaguar as the mysterious God of Night, sacred ruler of the underworld. Its spotted coat was said to represent the stars in the night sky. Jaguars were important to the Aztecs, who used animals as omens to help predict future events such as drought, war, death, and poverty. Preoccupied with battle, the Aztecs had great respect for such a large, powerful predator. They considered the jaguar the leader of all other animals—noble, cautious, proud, wise, and all-seeing, even in the dark. Only the bravest Aztec warriors could obtain the rank of jaguar and wear the cat's prestigious skin to designate their position.

The Jivaro Indians of northern Peru believe that shamans and chiefs can be transformed into young jaguars after dying. Mimicking the maternal care of a jaguar mother, they bring food to the body of a dead chief or shaman for two years—the same period of time it takes for a young jaguar to become fully independent. As a rite to manhood, the Yanomamo Indians of Venezuela paint their body with jaguar spots and chew leaves to hallucinate. The jaguar spirit was believed to have the strength of a powerful warrior.

Today, on the Yucatan peninsula at Palenque, behind the Temple of the Inscriptions, a steep trail leads through a patch of remnant rain forest to the overgrown Temple of the Jaguars. As the sacred animal of the shamans, the jaguar still

Opposite: Cryptically colored to blend into a shadowy forest environment, jaguars (*Panthera onca*) are skilled swimmers and tree climbers, most at home near streams, lakes, and rivers, where they often feed on caiman, turtles, tortoises, capybara, and fish.

Jaguars are the largest, strongest cat native to the Americas. Now extinct in the United States, jaguars range from Mexico to northern Argentina in South America. These cats are listed as endangered throughout their range, and only about a thousand are thought to remain in Mexico and Central America.

remains important in the religion and mythology of the Indians of Colombia. Among the Tarahumaras Indians of Mexico who lose sheep and goats to jaguars, it is said they refuse to hunt jaguars out of fear. Called *balam,* they were a sacred animal to the Mayas, who thought the sun hid inside the jaguar at night, taking on the cat's attributes to make nocturnal journeys into *Xibalba,* the Underworld.

Filled with jaguar symbolism, the Mayan religion, dating back to 2400 B.C., included an order of jaguar priests noted for their prophetic abilities. Mayan shamans transformed themselves into the shape of jaguars, and jaguars were associated with the Maya's bloodletting and sacrifice of both animals and humans to renew their people's connection with their ancestors and gods and the sacred cycle of life. Jaguar altars, apparently used in such sacrificial rituals, have been found at both Tikal in Guatemala and Chichen Itza in the Yucatan. The jaguar's skin, representing courage, ferocity, and leadership, symbolized all chieftains and was used to cover their seats of office. At night, a jaguar deity's pelt spread across the heavens to form the night sky, its spots twinkling as bright stars.

Of all the large cats, the jaguar is the least known to make unprovoked attacks on people and has never been officially documented as a man-eater. Some attacks have been provoked by hunters who have wounded a jaguar or harassed it with dogs. Jaguars sometimes follow people out of curiosity, patrolling human roads and fields, even climbing over trucks and road gear at night.

Nocturnal and nearly invisible behind a screen of mesmerizing spots, jaguars prefer dense cover, hunting at dawn, dusk, and during shadowy, moonlit nights. The name "jaguar" is thought to derive from *yaguara,* a South American word meaning "the wild beast that can kill its prey in a single bound." With nocturnal vision six times better than that of humans, retractable claws, piercing canines, and bodies built for stealth and ambush, jaguars are adept solitary predators, able to hunt and kill their prey alone.

Jaguars, like lions, can roar, but not purr. Their call has been compared to the single bark of a large dog followed by hoarse, coughlike growling. Females produce a rapid succession of coughing roars. The roars produced by males are slower in succession and more resounding. Among secretive, solitary cats such as the jaguar, vocalizations are important in attracting mates and avoiding direct aggressive contact.

Jaguars are solitary, except during the breeding season when males and females temporarily pair. Since the young remain with the female for at least two years, males must search large areas in order to find available mates. Males are much larger than females and—felid style—their courtship can be rough. One to four spotted kittens are born following a 110-day gestation period. Blind at birth, their eyes open after thirteen days. By six to eight weeks of age, the young are able to accompany their mother. Jaguars reach sexual maturity at three years. It is during dispersal from their natal area that males have a tough time. They run the risk of encountering resident males while crossing unfamiliar territory.

The jaguar's luxurious yellowish-brown fur marked with rosettes and spots provides camouflage in the jungle habitat, but makes it a highly prized target for the illegal trade in cat skins. Jaguars are baited, then spotlighted, and shot at night. Hunters also use "jaguar callers" that mimic a jaguar's guttural grunting to lure the curious cats within gunshot range. The tragedy of poaching is that such beautiful, intelligent animals could fall victim to an illegal trade featuring bribery and smuggling. The jaguar's habitat is also endangered as construction of airstrips for oil exploration and mining, new roads crisscrossing the Amazon basin, like the Trans-Amazonian Highway, and clearing for agriculture and settlement make once remote areas accessible to hunters and developers.

Jaguars attack dogs, horses, cattle, and other livestock when their natural prey base is eliminated; however, the number of cattle killed by jaguars is a small fraction of the number lost to parasites, floods, disease, and other natural factors. Very often, cattle-killers are created by people when gunshot wounds prevent a crippled jaguar from stalking its normal prey. It is a no-win situation for carnivores such as these, that need enormous tracts of undisturbed habitat in order to find necessary prey and mates, establish territories, and maintain adequate genetic diversity in their gene pool. In addition to the illegal trade in cat skins, trade in turtle meat and caiman skins has put jaguars in further competition with people for two of their food resources.

Since 1972, jaguars have been listed as endangered under the U.S. Endangered Species Act.

Overleaf: **Jaguars have the most powerful bite of all big cats, due to their jaw musculature and highly developed teeth. They typically kill large prey with a bite to the head, neck, or throat, dislocating and crushing neck vertebrae or puncturing the skull directly with their canines.**

The cougar is shy
and secretive,
typically avoiding
people in spite of
its large size. In
North America,
deer and elk are its
preferred prey.

They are listed in Appendix 1 of the 1973 Convention on International Trade in Endangered Species (CITES), which bans commercial trade in jaguars, live or in part. They are rare or absent from much of their former range. In November 1990, the Cockscomb Basin Wildlife Sanctuary in Belize—the only designated jaguar preserve in the world—was expanded by government decree to more than 100,000 acres, thirty times its initial size. Meanwhile, jaguars are continuing to lose ground due to poaching, often dubious elimination as pests, and habitat loss. It has been said that when the jaguar no longer walks the forests, there will never be anything like it again on earth.

PUMA/COUGAR/MOUNTAIN LION

Felis concolor

Tawny puffs of smoke able to break a bull's neck and yet so secretive.

—JIM KJELGAARD, *Lion Hound, 1955*

Seemingly invisible, the omnipresent but rarely seen cougar is not only the most widely distributed New World cat, but definitely the one with the most names. Depending on geographic region, it is called the puma, mountain lion, red tiger, deercat, mountain devil, king cat, Mexican lion, panther, mountain screamer, silver lion, catamount, even sneak cat.

Found from the Canadian Yukon to the tip of South America, from sea level to fourteen thousand feet or more, these adaptable, tawny cats have the greatest distribution of any terrestrial mammal in the Western Hemisphere—a range that extends over 110 degrees latitude. Equally at home in coniferous and tropical forests, prairies, deserts, and swamps, the cougar is a cryptic, elusive survivor doing its best to avoid contact with people.

At least one of their many names is the result of their surprising range of vocalizations. Although they cannot roar, cougars have been known to chirp, peep, even whistle. Kittens make a series of short, high-pitched peeps when frightened and adults sometimes produce low, hunting whistles before a chase. The name, screamer,

refers to the blood-curdling mating calls produced by a female cougar in estrus.

Long and lean, cougars are efficient day- and night-active predators built to leap, climb trees, sprint, and ambush. Reaching lengths of eight to nine feet and weights between eighty and two hundred pounds, cougars have excellent vision, hearing, and olfaction and use these senses to detect and stalk their prey. Long hind limbs in proportion to fore limbs are an adaptation for jumping and easier movement through steep canyons and ravines. Big, padded paws help the cougar navigate through variable terrain and grapple their next meal. Inch-and-a-half-long canines in concert with sheathed claws make them armed and deadly. Moving its head back and forth as it patrols its home range, a cougar uses its eyes to hunt, scanning for movement. When prey is detected, the eyes and ears of the cougar fix on the site until the source of motion is determined. With their long tail used for balance, these athletic felines can make incredible leaps in pursuit of prey or to silently disappear into the underbrush.

Although cougars prefer to eat deer and elk, their generalist diet can include everything from mouse to moose, including grasshoppers. When larger animals are not available, they prey on smaller fare such as rabbits, raccoons, feral pigs, bats, frogs, and rodents. During his study of

Above: Symbolic of the untamed West and all things wild, the cougar (*Felis concolor*) has a renegade presence, both real and imagined.

Pumas (*Felis concolor*) that inhabit the tropical rain forests of Central and South America are almost never seen in the wild. As a result, very little is known about their feeding habits or range.

cougars in the Salmon River Mountains of Idaho, John Seidensticker documented the fact that both solitary male and female cougars kill adult male elk. This is a remarkable feat considering that bulls weigh seven times more than a female cougar. It underscores the fact that most of us have inaccurate perceptions about the intelligence and predatory skills of these golden cats.

Cougars kill large ungulates by leaping onto their backs from a position of ambush. By grasping the back of the elk's neck with its canines, and pulling the elk's head back with its powerful forelegs, the cougar can snap an elk's neck. Mule deer have been found that were killed by a single crushing bite to the base of the skull. To prevent coyotes, eagles, and ravens from scavenging their kills, cougars often bury the carcass, covering it with sticks and leaves. In this manner, they are able to feed from a large kill for several days.

As the only other plain-colored big cat besides the African lion, cougars come in a variety of shades. In tropical areas, their coat tends to be more reddish-brown. Further north, their fur lightens to silver-gray. In between they can be sandy brown or buff, depending on habitat. Soft as sable, their fur has been described as smelling clean and wild, almost sweet.

When the first explorers arrived in the New World, they reported seeing "lions" in Central and South America, as well as in the early colonies. Although these big American cats are the same color, with both sexes resembling the maneless African lioness, they are not true lions. Unlike their social relatives from the Dark Continent, cougars do not form prides, hunt in a group, or share their prey. However, through a comparative study of their molecular genetics, it was revealed that cougars are more closely allied with the big cats in the pantherine group rather than with the small cats. Genetic analysis also indicates that they may share ancestry with the extinct cheetah-like cats that roamed North America up to ten thousand years ago.

Felis concolor, the "cat of one color," once inhabited the entire continental United States. Two thousand years ago, its range was probably continuous from southeastern Alaska south to Tierra del Fuego. Since 1900, cougar populations across this north-south distribution have been eliminated due to hunting, habitat loss, and effective predator control campaigns. In the United States, only about half of their historic range remains. An estimated sixteen to twenty thousand "ghostwalkers" survive in the mountain and desert regions of the western United States and in parts of southern Texas.

Now considered predominantly a western animal, cougars have become a symbol of the last wilderness frontier. Just 150 years ago they were more common east of the Mississippi in the eastern deciduous forests where they preyed on white-tailed deer. Now, despite numerous, undocumented sightings of cougars in New

Opposite: **The cougar (*Felis concolor*), mountain lion, or puma is called many different names depending on geographic location. It ranges from the Canadian Yukon to the tip of South America, from sea level to fourteen thousand feet, in forests, deserts, and swamps. Rarely seen in any environment, this elusive cat has also been called the ghostwalker.**

England, the eastern cougar survives only as a relict population at the tip of Florida—extremely rare, inbred, and classified as an endangered subspecies.

As the largest free-ranging cat in North America, the cougar figures prominently in Native American folklore. The Great Lakes tribes believed that their tails whipped up the waves and storms on the lakes. Cherokee Indians called them *klandagi,* "lord of the forest," and the Chickasaws called them *ko-icto,* "cat of god." The Cochiti Indians of New Mexico carved life-sized stone statues of cougars and built shrines in their honor, and the ancient city of Cuzco in Peru is said to have been laid out in the shape of a cougar. So revered was the big cat by many Native Americans in southern California that Christian missionaries found such beliefs an obstacle in trying to establish new missions. The native people refused to kill the amber cats or protect their livestock from attack.

Reverence aside, cougars ultimately faced the same fate as all large American predators— they were classified as vermin. An early report from the provincial British Columbia Game Commission (1906) best describes their early status: "When the amount of game one of these animals [cougars] killed in a year and its value to the country is taken into consideration, it must be admitted that even if a few thousand dollars has to be expended every year in their extermination, the money would be well invested."

During the early to mid-1900s, British Columbia paid bounties ranging from $15 to $40 for a dead cougar. The bounty system was part of a predator-destruction program based on a belief that cougars destroyed livestock and competed for game animals and birds. Bounties were set to encourage public pursuit of the felines. They worked. In one year 456 cougars were killed on Vancouver Island alone. The excavation of large tracts of wilderness through logging helped expedite the elimination process. Paid, full-time predator hunters replaced the bounty system in 1957. In the United States, similar predator control efforts were waged against the cougar in just about every western state.

Only in 1969 did the first major publication on the ecology of cougars first appear in print. It was the result of a pioneering field study conducted by Maurice Hornocker in the rugged Idaho Primitive Area. Together with friend and research partner Wilber Wiles, Hornocker managed to capture sixty-four different cougars in a two-hundred-square-mile area of isolated wilderness—not once, but more than three hundred times during the ten-year study.

Scientists learn a great deal about the feeding habits of wild cats by studying their scats. Fresh carnivore scats are initially black, but weather to white with age. Not only is the age of a scat quickly apparent, but so are its contents. Close inspection of the incompletely digested material such as hair and bone fragments can reveal what a cat had for dinner.

Field studies have shown that cougars are typically solitary, spending most of their lives in well-defined home ranges that vary in size according to a cat's gender, the season, habitat quality, and prey availability. Generally, male territories are larger than those of females, with females often sharing overlapping ranges. For breeding access, male territories may overlap several female ranges, but never those of other resident males. Cougars mark the boundaries of their territories with olfactory signposts, or scrapes, specifically by building and urinating on piles of dirt, pine needles, and leaves. In search of home ranges, young and transient cougars are allowed to travel through the established ranges of resident cats, but not to tarry long.

Following a ninety- to ninety-five-day gestation period, females produce up to six blue-eyed cubs covered with dark brown spots. At birth, each weighs a pound or less, a mere fraction of their mother's eighty- to one-hundred-thirty-pound weight. The cubs nurse for three or more months, but begin to eat meat at six weeks of age. This means the female must kill two to three times as much prey to fuel the energy demands of lactation, as well as to satisfy the quick-growing cubs' need for fresh meat. By six months, the cubs weigh thirty to forty pounds and their spots begin to disappear. At sixteen months their eyes turn greenish yellow. Cubs remain with the female for eighteen to twenty-four months. After leaving her, littermates often hunt and travel together for a few more months before dispersing.

Research on captive-reared cougars has shown that kittens will not kill a potential prey species unless they have fed on it before the encounter. Cougar kittens imprint to prey on those species that their mother has captured.

Opposite: Until the 1960s, bounties were posted on cougars in Canada and the United States, where they were shot, trapped, and poisoned as vermin. Only after field research showed the importance of large predators in the balance of natural ecosystems did attitudes begin to change.

While cases have been reported of a female cougar accompanied by cubs killing as many as 100 lambs in an evening—eating none—and a female bobcat in northern Georgia killing as many as 125 turkeys in an evening—eating only one, or none—such rare events have been attributed to overzealous moms eager to teach their cubs the fine art of killing prey. It now appears that in many areas, cougars do not feed on livestock at all. In other hot spots, such as a few places in Arizona, cougars survive by utilizing calves for 30 to 35 percent of their diet.

At the insistence of ranchers in southeastern Arizona, the Animal Damage Control (ADC), an agency with the U.S. Department of Agriculture, shot and trapped fifty cats over several thousand acres in Graham County between 1988 and 1990. As an end-product of this weeding program, the ADC gave eleven decapitated cougar heads to the Arizona Game and Fish Department as a routine data sample. The heads would have gathered dust and the cats never been missed if a disgusted Game and Fish employee hadn't documented the event. He stacked the heads into a grisly pyramid against a tree trunk, photographed the monument to dead cougars, and then widely distributed the photograph in protest to ADC's actions.

The resulting protest from environmental groups inspired a three-year study of radio-collared cougars by the Arizona Game and Fish Department in a 360-square-mile area of ranches. The dramatic photo forced everyone to look for better solutions. For example, in Idaho, ranchers successfully move their cattle to safer pastures during the calving season, removing temptation from the cougars. In Arizona, the ADC is making more of an effort to identify individual animals that are troublesome rather than eliminating all possible suspects.

Maurice Hornocker points out that taxpayers spend more money controlling cattle-eating cougars in a few isolated circumstances than ranchers ever lose to cat-related predation. Field studies now indicate that killing off cougars through predator-control efforts often backfires when vacant territories are created for transient, inexperienced cougars. In fact, a long-term study of cougar predation on bighorn sheep, made by Hornocker at the White Sands Missile Range in New Mexico, has shown that predation decreases as cougar populations are allowed to stabilize by leaving the cats alone. Deer populations are healthier when these carnivores are allowed to cull the weak and sick.

In the meantime, cougars are still shot on sight by unhappy ranchers in southern Arizona, and Texas allows unrestrained cougar killing. In Utah, interest in the sport of cougar hunting is increasing, as reflected by the growing number of pursuit permits being issued each year. During the 1993–1994 season, the available permits were increased from 525 to 666. While the remaining states with cougar populations allow the controlled seasonal hunting of cougars as game animals, California is the only state that, so far, has won a hard-fought battle to eliminate sport hunting for cougar altogether.

"The lion plays a tremendous role in wilderness ecosystems," says Hornocker. "It sits at the absolute apex of the food chain. It is an indicator of the health of the ecosystem and helps maintain the stability of the system."

According to Donald Schueler in his 1991 book *Incident at Eagle Ranch*, "the mountain lion works a strong magic in the imagination of many Americans. It is the ultimate loner, a renegade presence in the wildest canyons and wildest mountains, the sign of everything that is remote from us, everything we have not spoiled."

FLORIDA PANTHER

Felis concolor coryi

Called the panther, or painter, these extremely secretive, solitary, tawny-colored felines are one of the most difficult American animals to see in the wild. They are also one of the most endangered. Their small feet, long legs, darker color, light weight, and white flecking around the neck distinguish them from other cougar subspecies. Once found throughout the entire southeastern United States, only thirty to fifty Florida panthers remain in the hardwood hammocks and remote cypress swamps of southern Florida, mostly in the Everglades and Big Cypress Swamp ecosystems.

Sixty years ago, 200,000 white ibis, tricolored herons, wood storks, and other water birds nested here. Ten years ago their numbers had dropped to nine thousand. Today, just two to four thousand remain. Their reduced numbers are silent testimony to the success of the Central and Southern Florida Flood Control Project,

Man-Eating Cats

THE MEAT OF MYTH AND LEGEND

The blood more stirs to rouse a lion than to start a hare.

—WILLIAM SHAKESPEARE, *Henry IV*

Above: **Undoubtedly the most notorious of man-eaters, tigers (*Panthera tigris*) have killed thousands of people on the subcontinent of India. Today such attacks are prompted more often from loss of prey and habitat than from a specific desire for human flesh.**

Opposite: **Nothing can be as unnerving as the predatory gaze of a big cat, especially when directed at you. Here a jaguar (*Panthera onca*) peers through the rain forest vegetation.**

Art historian Robert McCracken Peck, a fellow of the Academy of Natural Sciences of Philadelphia, best captured the hair-raising essense of being stalked by a man-eating cat when he described Charles R. Knight's famous painting, "Danger Under the Moon": "In a haunting scene that is both ancient and timeless," wrote Peck, "a human family seeks shelter for the night. The weary man, comforted by his spear and fire, dozes from his watch while his mate and child sleep quietly in the shelter of a cave. Above them in the moonlight, silent and invisible from where they rest, a murky form takes shape. It is a cat—the threatening, thrilling, mystical power of wilderness itself" (*International Wildlife*, September/October 1991).

Since the Pleistocene (2 million to 10,000 years ago), large cats and humans have co-evolved in intelligence and weaponry as the planet's top terrestrial predators. In fact, efforts to avoid predation by carnivorous cats has probably had far greater influence on the evolution of early human intelligence and social structure than is credited. Superior in size, strength and agility, the big cats were finally outcompeted by a collective human intelligence that produced machines, weapons, and more impermeable shelters. Yet remove these high-tech trappings, let a person wander unarmed into big-cat territory by day or night, and *Homo sapiens* is once again no match for a large feline.

"If we concentrate our imagination on a giant feline form," wrote British ethologist Desmond Morris (*Big Cats of the World*, 1975), "hurtling towards us through the air, its flick-knife claws spread naked from its padded feet, its limb-muscles tense for a stunning blow, its crunching jaws impatient to plunge home its dagger teeth, we can be excused if, even in the warm security of our beds, we feel a wave of primeval panic pass through our bodies."

According to Michael Robinson, director of the National Zoo in Washington, D.C., "an arms race implies a dynamism between attack and defense" (*Smithsonian*, April 1992). Take, for example, the zebra's stripes, in part an optical defense against big cats. In turn, felines have evolved their own cryptic stripes and spots to confuse the

Opposite: **When a pair of male lions near Kenya's Tsavo River began preying on the Indian railroad workers in 1898, construction came to a grinding halt for three weeks until they could be shot. Considered more brazen than man-eating tigers, for their habit of entering villages and pulling victims from tents, man-eating lions most recently caused problems in Tanzania.**

visual perception of prey species. Finally, the feline eye has been perfected for nocturnal vision; it is six times better than that of humans. Operating like infrared spotting scopes, a cat's eyes can see a nighttime world kept invisible to us by darkness.

The dynamics between early hominids and large carnivorous felines is a classic predator-prey relationship. Robinson points out that the thorn fence, or *boma,* used around villages in Africa, is a defense strategy that utilizes the antipredator adaptation of thorny plants to keep nocturnal lions and leopards at bay. Such protective walls around human habitations have been used since prehistoric times. In fact, until the mid-1600s, more resources were typically invested in defensive walls than in all other public works combined.

Vegetable barbed wire aside, prehistoric felines undoubtedly influenced the evolution of early humans. Fossil evidence indicates that leopards were contemporaneous with early hominids and shared the same habitats. Puncture marks found on the fossil cranial bones of baboons and early hominids show that leopards have long featured us as a protein supplement. Using this evidence, and the observation of modern leopard-primate relationships, leopard specialist John Cavallo (*Natural History,* February 1990) proposed that our early ancestors had a predatory-parasitic relationship with leopards. By day, tree-stored leopard kills may have provisioned scavenging hominids with meat, skins, and bone marrow. At night, leopards turned the table and stalked our ancestors—as they still do baboons, chimpanzees, and *Homo sapiens.*

According to biologist Randall Eaton (*The World's Cats,* 1976), "it was only when man could dominate competing grouped predators, that intraspecific competition between groups of hominids could accelerate the evolution of technology and warfare. Perhaps reciprocity between unrelated groups—the keystone of hominid evolution—was initially favored because of its advantages in competition with grouped predators. If so, interspecific competition between our ancestors and lions may have been the last and most important obstacle to the evolution of civilization."

Man-eating cats continue to have a profound effect on human behavior. When tigers killed more than four hundred people near Bhiwapur, India, in 1769, the town was abandoned. During

Lieutenant-Colonel Jim Corbett's days hunting man-eating cats in India, he described an entire village boarded shut and residents held captive inside for five days by a marauding tigress. In Kenya, during construction of the East African Railroad, a pair of healthy man-eating lions killed so many laborers during a nine-month period that construction had to be halted for three

In recent years more than a hundred people have been killed by man-eating tigers near Dudwa National Park. Indian conservationist Billy Arjan Singh blames people, not tigers. According to Singh, the attacks were provoked by an invasion of villagers cutting grass and collecting firewood in the tiger reserve, and by the planting of tall sugarcane around its periphery. The cane fields, similar to the tiger's normal grassland habitat, provide ideal habitat for females raising cubs, as well as cover from which to ambush people who wander through the area.

A stable territory is especially important for a female with cubs. She must provision her young with food until they are about a year-and-a-half old. Finding enough food for herself and two or three 250-pound cubs is no simple task. Familiarization with the best places to hunt, rest, and find water are the advantages of a stable territory. Habitat destruction plays havoc with such systems.

"Very few reserves and national parks are large enough to contain wild cats," says carnivore specialist Paul Joslin. "This forces most wide-ranging felines to survive outside park boundaries—in direct conflict with people."

Such conflicts are bound to increase as human and livestock populations swell around shrinking tiger habitat. Long-term tiger studies have shown that loss of home range can trigger some man-eating activity. As with exclusive real estate, there are only a limited number of available tiger territories. With effective conservation efforts and increased survival of tigers, the number of tigers in need of home range exceeds the vacancy rate. Wildlife corridors connecting protected forest would help relieve this pressure. When none exist, young tigers are forced into greater contact—and conflict—with people and livestock. When local people begin to ask the question "Are tigers more important than humans?" a backlash against conservation efforts can ensue if human needs for protection are not met as well.

attack their victims from behind, Ram concluded that eyes on the back of one's head might intimidate the man-eating cats. Rubber masks of human faces with big eyes were designed for that purpose and distributed to the local people in 1986. Of the thirty people killed by tigers the following year, none were wearing the masks when they were attacked.

LEOPARDS

During a visit to Zambia's Kafue National Park—in which we were chased by a herd of elephants—game warden Cecil Evans was emphatic that visitors stay in their vehicles. "The animals here are wild," he warned, "very, very wild." To

Even if they are not full-fledged man-eaters, wild lions are unpredictable and dangerous. Tourists have been attacked by lions when they got out of their vehicles at the wrong place.

drive his point home, he told about a man who got out of his Land Rover to briefly "use" the park bushes—and was attacked by a leopard hidden *in* the bushes.

"Leopards are incredibly bold and clever like a coyote," says Pat Quillen of SOS-Care. "They are too smart. I don't trust them. Their expression stays the same, yet their minds are always working. Everything is a challenge to them—and they can have such rapid mood changes." As a

case in point, Quillen tells the story of Victor Huddleston, who hand-raised a female leopard in Missouri in the 1970s only to have her kill and partly eat him as an adult.

Ecologist Norman Myers (*International Wildlife,* November/December 1974) described the leopard as the most feline of the great cats—sinuous, stealthy, and stronger pound for pound than any other of the great predators. "A leopard on the prowl takes care to conceal itself from the start," he says, "while at the moment of attack it reveals itself for only a few moments—if that."

Colonel Jim Corbett, who spent a lifetime hunting man-eating cats in India, considered leopards the strongest and most skilled of wild animals, and definitely the most intelligent. When these high-I.Q. cats direct their nocturnal hunting skills toward human prey, they become especially deadly. Attacking people as they move about in the dark, or by stealing into their homes, a man-eating leopard can be as difficult to avoid as it is to capture.

According to author Peter Hathaway Capstick (*Maneaters,* 1981), "In the life and death contest between man and man-eater, in no other case is the human hunter more likely to end up as the killer's deliberate next meal as with the leopard. A man-eating leopard is the most difficult and dangerous of all cats to hunt because of its unnerving ability to reverse situations in its favor."

Several professional hunters succumbed to such talents while stalking one particular man-eating leopard in India. In a manner similar to the way leopards kill baboons in their sleeping trees at night, all were plucked right out of the tree blinds they set up to ambush the deadly cat. In this case, it almost appeared as if the wily leopard had used the remains from its last human kill to bait each of the hunters. As they watched the carcass, the leopard used the opportunity to stalk and kill them.

Fossil evidence shows that leopards have killed hominids since Australopithecines hunted and gathered in Africa. Their night-stalking habits undoubtedly helped influence our primordial fear of darkness and our need to gather close around a blazing fire. *Homo sapiens,* it would seem, has always been a normal part of the leopard's diet—along with all other species of primates endemic to its territory.

Much of what is known about man-eating leopards is due to the late, great hunter Jim Corbett. Two man-eating leopards of Kumaon killed 525 people between them before being shot by Corbett. Because leopards are opportunistic feeders—bordering on scavengers—Corbett believed some became man-eaters after dining on human corpses, later transferring the acquired taste to live prey. Severe epidemics that create a surplus of human corpses prove ideal for such transformations. This was true for the man-eating leopards of Kumaon. Their killing spree followed the influenza epidemic of 1918. Loss of the leopard's natural prey can also trigger man-eating.

When a leopard does develop a penchant for human flesh, the results can be frightening—because of the animal's ability to outwit people in a deadly game of cat and mouse. Under normal circumstances, leopards often enter villages to snatch dogs and other domestic creatures into the night. Man-eaters go one step further, entering homes to drag human victims from their hearths and beds.

One such bold leopard was the Rudraprayag man-eater of India that killed 125 people or more. Extremely clever at procuring victims, this notorious cat stole into a house, quietly grabbed a man by the throat, and dragged him across a room and through a doorway before the man he was sitting near realized the fatal attack had taken place. Only the cat's departing silhouette on the wall revealed the feline's silent, deadly presence.

LIONS

While tigers may be man-eaters supreme in Asia, African lions are equally dangerous and have killed their fair share of people. The same circumstances that turn big cats into livestock killers—old age, injuries, loss of natural habitat and prey—can convert a feline into a man-eater. As wild lands are converted to agriculture and human settlements, food chains are disrupted, forcing large predators such as the lion and tiger into greater contact with livestock, and ultimately, people.

The best example of this occurred recently in southern Tanzania. Because tsetse flies have eliminated most cattle and other domestic animals in the area, the local people have turned to wildlife for meat, leaving little for the lions. With their natural prey eliminated, the lions have aggressively turned to people. A ten-year-old boy was killed as he slept in his bed. As the rest of the family hid in adjoining rooms, the lion stayed until dawn, leisurely eating its meal.

Man-eating lions can be much more aggressive than tigers in pursuit of human prey, often employing the same cooperative hunting strategies used to bring down zebras and antelopes. The Tsavo man-eaters entered railroad cars to attack people. Another lion pulled a man from his horse and dragged him sixty yards. Others have broken through hut roofs, torn off doors, and broken into tents to get their victims.

Several years ago in Kenya, a woman tourist on safari with her husband was attacked near her parked car. In 1974, professional hunter Peter Hankin was killed with a single bite to his neck as he lay in his tent. The lioness then settled down to eat him, as safari clients in nearby tents spent a sleepless night listening to the morbid sounds. According to Peter Capstick (*Maneaters*, 1981), if you are going to get yourself killed by a man-eating lion, the best time to do so, with the least complications, is while sleeping. Give a thoughtless lurch at the last minute, he adds, and you could be dragged off to an eternity of unpleasant moments.

People are not the only type of primates stalked by lions. In Tanzania's Mahali Mountains National Park, chimp hair, teeth, and bones were discovered in lion feces soon after two adolescent males and two adult female chimps disappeared from a study group. This discovery explains why lion calls can send chimps into a tizzy—they whimper, give alarm calls, and climb trees. The recycled chimp parts were the first definitive proof that lions eat chimpanzees.

Captive lions can be equally dangerous. An employee at Lion Country Safari in West Palm Beach, California, was severely mauled by a 450-pound male lion who attacked her after pushing open a steel door that had not been securely closed. The lion severed her jugular vein and inflicted other puncture wounds that caused both her lungs to collapse. She survived by shutting herself into a nearby cage—followed by emergency surgery.

Two lions recently killed a twenty-four-year-old German tourist in Etosha National Park, Namibia, after he decided to spend the night in a sleeping bag near a water hole. The male and female that ambushed the man were both in very poor condition, which probably prompted the attack. Both lions were subsequently tranquilized and put to sleep.

In Botswana's Okavango, an American tourist was grabbed by the foot as she lay in a sleeping

Overleaf: When describing jaguars (*Panthera onca*), a distinction needs to be made between man-killing and man-eating cats. There are few, if any, reports of jaguars eating people.

bag outside her tent. A quick-witted guide ended up playing tug-of-war with the bold feline until it finally ran away with the sleeping bag—sans tourist.

JAGUARS AND CHEETAHS

Considering their size, it is remarkable that there are not more verified stories of jaguar attacks on people. For this species, a distinction needs to be made between man-killing and man-eating cats. While there are numerous verified reports of jaguars attacking people, some provoked, there are few, if any, of jaguars actually eating people. There are many stories of people being followed undisturbed for miles through the jungle by these curious cats.

Cheetahs have never been known to attack people without a cause. They are considered to be the most shy and gentle of all wild cats.

COUGARS

In 1990, medical student Lynda Walters came face-to-face with a mountain lion on a trail in Four-Mile Canyon west of Boulder, Colorado. The big cat not only stalked her, but was joined by a second cougar with the same intentions. Yelling and rock throwing did not discourage the cats, and neither did climbing twelve feet up into a ponderosa pine. One of the cats came after Walters, cutting two 6-inch slashes down the back of her right calf. She kicked one cat in the head and used a branch spear to keep the second at bay. Only at sunset, when the cats departed to drink in a nearby creek, did Walters leave the tree to run a mile to her parents' house.

Since 1986 more than four hundred lion sightings and encounters have occurred in the Boulder, Colorado, area. Seemingly omnipresent, the lions have shown up in schoolyards, backyards, within city limits, even downtown. Many are oblivious to cars, lawn mowers, and noisy kids. Some walk right down the middle of roads. There have been increased sightings of lions traveling together, and at lower elevations. In fact, nowhere in the country have mountain lions been seen as frequently.

Mountain lions hunt with their mothers until they are twelve to eighteen months old. At that time, they become solitary hunters, called "transients," in search of their own home range. Studies suggest that due to habitat restrictions, it is the transient lions that have the most trouble with people. With available lion territories saturated, transients are forced to move into more suburban areas.

According to Colorado hunting guide Don Justman, such cougars have been forced to modify their behavior in order to cope and survive. "If the mountain lion takes someone's cocker spaniel off the front porch," says Justman, "he's made it through another day" (*Los Angeles Times Magazine,* March 1, 1992).

In 1991 a mountain lion jumped and killed an eighteen-year-old jogger on a trail near his high school in Idaho Springs, Colorado. The lion pulled him down from behind and crushed his neck. In British Columbia, two children and a woman were clawed by a young lion. That same year, Orange County lost a lawsuit and was forced to pay $2 million to the family of an El Toro girl who received severe eye, head, and leg injuries during a lion attack in Ronald W. Caspers Wilderness Park. The park has since been closed to minors as a result.

According to statistics on mountain lion attacks compiled by wildlife ecologist Paul Beier (*Los Angeles Times Magazine,* March 1, 1992), there were eleven fatalities and forty-nine reported injuries to people from these cats in Canada and America between 1890 and 1990. Several deaths have been caused by cougar attacks on Vancouver Island, where all the victims have been children. In 1992 an eight-year-old boy was fatally mauled by a cougar as he sat on the grass in the elementary school playground at Kyuquot, a remote Indian community on the island. The cougar rushed from the forest bordering the playground and pounced on the child.

The dramatic death of a forty-year-old woman jogger in April 1994 called greater attention to the growing presence of these day-active carnivores. While running the Auburn Lake Trails near Cool, California, Barbara Schoener was fatally attacked and partly eaten just northeast of Sacramento. As human populations increase and invade mountain lion habitat, especially for recreational purposes during the summer months, the chances of a random attack by a starving or wounded cougar also increase. "An empty stomach is a strong motivating factor," says California Department of Fish and Game warden Larry Bruckenstein.

In the late 1960s, to limit excessive hunting, California declared mountain lions protected game mammals. Then, in 1990, voters passed Proposition 117, which permanently banned sport hunting the big cats and increased fines for poaching them. Only when a mountain lion takes to killing livestock or harming people can a "depredation permit" be issued, which gives permission to destroy the cat. Prior to 1982, only one to five such permits were issued a year. In 1993, sixty were requested and used.

When one such brazen cougar was killed after it had taken a fancy to a man's sheep, state wildlife officials discovered parts of a family cat, sheep, and a missing Peking duck. Mountain lions usually prey on deer, jackrabbits, and domestic dogs and cats—but with loss of habitat, they have become bolder. As a result, many ranchers have abandoned sheep for more cougar-proof cattle.

According to an Olympic National Park handout on "Traveling in Cougar Country," the mountain lion is a large and potentially dangerous animal that is common but infrequently seen. Attacks on humans are rare—unsupervised children and lone adults tend to be most at risk. Persons running or moving rapidly are also at higher risk. Because more cougar attacks have occurred in the western United States and Canada during the past twenty years than in the previous eighty, rangers advise that you hike in small groups rather than alone, stay alert to your surroundings, and avoid approaching dead animals. Most important, keep your children under close control and leave your cougar-attracting pets at home.

So what should you do if you come face-to-face with a mountain lion? First, don't panic. Pick up small children immediately. Face the cat, maintain direct eye contact and stay upright. Cats typically move in to attack when you aren't looking—or when you turn to flee, triggering a chase-and-pounce response. Do not approach the cat. It's best to move away slowly without turning your back on the feline. The trick is to convince the predator that you are dangerous—not dinner—so make yourself look as big as possible by raising your arms and jacket above your head and staying on higher ground than the cougar. If the cat persists, yell, throw rocks and sticks, wave your arms, and if necessary, fight back aggressively.

"With bears you can play dead," explains Dennis Pemble, a wildlife-control officer for the B.C. Ministry of Environment. "But if you do that with a cougar, you are going to *be dead*. Cougars do not attack because they are mad. They attack because they want to eat you" (*Los Angeles Times Magazine*, March 1, 1992).

What should you do if you end up eye-to-eye with a wild cougar? First remember—as your heart beats out of your chest—that more people have died from encounters with dogs, bees, snakes, and deer than encounters with mountain lions. It should also be comforting to know that rattlesnakes, not cougars, bite five thousand people each year.

While normally shy and retiring, a few cougars (*Felis concolor*) have recently taken to stalking people, particularly young children and joggers, who seem to trigger a cat-and-mouse response. Anyone visiting cougar country is advised to contact park rangers to learn safe ways to share the cats' habitat.

4

The Elusive Small Cats

The smallest feline is a masterpiece.

—*Leonardo Da Vinci*

Although not as dramatic as the great cats—tigers, lions, leopards, and jaguars— the many species of secretive smaller cats are as beautiful as they are important to predator-prey relationships. Holding the basic felid body plan constant, they have radiated along the dimension of size into a host of predators needed to keep various prey populations in check. Small cats help control crop-raiding birds and rodents, invading rabbits, and rodents that spread disease. As important ecosystem managers, these intriguing, mostly nocturnal felids occupy every conceivable niche.

Included in this wonderful felid radiation are species with webbed toes that pursue aquatic prey; arboreal gymnasts that can dangle from a tree branch by one foot; big-eared cats that stalk desert sand dunes; and cats with snowshoes for feet. There are even a couple of species that like to dive into water, one that prowls caves for bats, and others that make a living by leaping high off the ground to snatch prey from the air. And not to be overlooked is the behaviorally plastic domestic cat—an opportunist *par excellence,* that has accompanied man to the far corners of the Earth.

Little cats are different from the bigger cats in more ways than just size. When bright light shines on their eyes, their pupils close to slits. In contrast, the pupils of their larger cousins close to circles. Only the great cats can roar. The bones inside a small cat's voice box are connected so tightly that only small vibrations are possible.

Felines are the planet's most widely distributed group of mammals, yet as carnivores at the top of their food chains, they have never been plentiful. Now they are in serious trouble. Some small felids are simply, quietly, disappearing due to habitat loss. Others are taken for their fur, for sport, or for medicinal purposes. Still others are killed as vermin, kept illegally as pets, or eaten by people. In some areas, felines continue to die accidentally, killed on roads that transect their territories.

"Since 1600," says carnivore specialist Paul Joslin, "half of all mammalian species that have gone extinct are predators. They are rare to start with—rarer than prey—making them extremely vulnerable. They are typically the first to go" (*Animals,* July/August 1991).

Above: One of the most beautiful small cats, the margay (*Felis wiedii*) uses its enormous eyes to help navigate arboreal pathways at night in the rain forests of South and Central America.

Opposite: A North American lynx (*Lynx canadensis*) in the Bob Marshall Wilderness Area of Montana uses its large padded feet to climb an aspen tree—and to stalk over deep snow.

125

The most common wild cat of southern Asia, the leopard cat (*Felis bengalensis*) is at home in dense tropical rain forests, as well as in scrub and semidesert areas. Although no bigger than a house cat, leopard cats are hunted for food, stuffed as tourist trophies, and killed to provide spotted pelts to the Asian fur market.

Yet if these cats do go, scientists point out, animals that share their ecosystems may soon follow. Considered umbrella species that keep other species in check, these mostly night-stalking carnivores have had a significant influence on the evolution, behavior, and ecology of their vertebrate prey—even though as meat-eaters they represent less than 1 percent of the world's four thousand mammalian species.

"With their reliance on a meat diet," explains Gary Koehler (*Natural History*, December 1988) "their generally solitary nature, and often a need for large home ranges, many felids are less able than other predators to cope with changes in their environment, especially those brought about by humans. Their relatively low reproductive rate—producing fewer young but investing more energy rearing each one—is also better suited to stable conditions. For the most part, cats do not cope well with change, and as a result, trapping, trophy hunting, and habitat destruction have pushed many of the world's cats to the brink of extinction."

In 1972, when the first endangered species list was published, more than 50 percent of the small felid species indigenous to South America were already considered endangered or threatened by extinction. Asia has the highest diversity of felids of any area in the world, yet its rain forests are also under siege.

Ultimately, if wild cats are to survive, not only must habitat destruction be slowed, but successful captive breeding programs need to be established. This seems simple enough, except for two problems: habitat destruction is accelerating, and most species of small felids do not breed well in captivity. It appears that noise, lack of privacy, proximity to large numbers of people, and other disturbances inhibit the captive reproduction of these shy, secretive carnivores.

Under the best of conditions, felid reproduction has been described as a fine line between mating and killing. In captivity, with no escape, these dynamics become exaggerated. "Animals, often pairs, may have been living peacefully, or at least in tolerable armistice, together for years,"

says Paul Leyhausen, "yet suddenly one kills the other." Should litters be produced, the male may target the young as prey, or the female may kill them herself, or simply abandon them. Hand-rearing baby carnivores is not easy. Many felid cubs contract incurable diarrhea if they are fed whole cow's milk.

The bottom line is: How do you keep such intelligent, physically active, typically solitary animals happy enough to breed in captivity? In the wild, felines perpetually patrol their large territories. Ocelots cross and recross their home range in search of prey, sometimes crossing their entire range every two to four days. In captivity this can translate into endless pacing behavior throughout limited enclosures. With extreme sensitivity to human disturbance, and anatomy and brain power evolved to stalk, outwit, and ambush prey, it's little wonder that so many wild cats do not breed well in captivity—much less that they occasionally kill each other. Zoos are doing the best they can to help protect these exotic cats, but life in captivity—for better and worse—just isn't the same as life in the wild.

"When I first went to the libraries to learn about small felids," says Pat Quillen of SOS, CARE, Inc., "I found virtually nothing had been written about them. They had literally fallen through the cracks of scientific study." Since then, Quillen has successfully bred and maintained dozens of endangered small wild cats—everything from desert cats, margays, ocelots, and sand cats to tigrinas, Geoffroy's, and leopard cats. After nearly three decades of research and devotion to the fifty or more small felines in her charge, Quillen has become as knowledgeable about small cats as she is articulate about the need to protect them.

Scientists became aware of the endangered status of many small spotted felids because of the drastic decline in the number of skins being traded annually. "The major concern," says Betsy Dresser, research director at the Cincinnati Zoo, "is that very little is known of the behavior and reproductive biology of the small felines—or of their status in the wild. Very few are safeguarded in captivity. In many cases, no censuses have ever been done on the small cats, and yet habitat is decreasing at such an alarming rate, it is now hard to determine what is going on. To save small cats, wild and captive observation is essential during the coming decade."

According to Norman Myers (*The World's Cats,* 1976), "This situation of 'don't know, can't say' has induced some observers to say that until there is positive evidence that things are going wrong, there is little reason to stop exploiting the cats." He adds later that "much depends on what is meant by 'endangered.' Perhaps one has to wait until a species is in the sort of trouble that requires not just special protection, but all-out efforts at greater expense in staff and money, not to mention time. Or perhaps one should move while the species is only in danger of danger."

Adds Paul Joslin (*Animals,* July/August 1991), "Wild felines play too great a service in pest control to be considered vermin." People kill wild cats to keep them from killing their domestic animals, but then lose valuable crops to uncontrolled feline prey, such as rodents. For example, a decline of small and medium-sized cats in Argentina resulted in a sharp increase in prey species, which led to decreased agricultural production. Having learned the hard way, we now know that predators must be maintained so as not to disrupt ecosystems.

"Cats," concludes Michael Robinson, director of the National Zoo in Washington, D.C., "are quintessentially part of the perfection of nature."

BOBCAT

Lynx rufus

SOUTHERN CANADA TO CENTRAL MEXICO

About twice the size of a large house cat, the ear-tufted, muttonchop bobcat is North America's most common native cat. Historically found coast to coast, from southern Canada to central America, these light gray to reddish-brown cats can be found in almost every area of the United States—from woodlands bordering eastern suburbs, the spruce forests of Maine and the swamps and forests of Florida, to the deserts and high mountains of the West—wherever there is adequate prey and plenty of places to hide. In fact, New York's Catskill Mountains were named after this omnipresent carnivore.

The "bob" refers to their short tails, a physical trait shared with their close relatives the lynx. They carry their black-tipped tails up in the air,

Opposite: Twice the size of a domestic cat, but with shorter legs and smaller feet than a lynx, bobcats (*Lynx rufus*) inhabit forests and deserts from southern Canada to central Mexico. Rabbits, jackrabbits, and snowshoe hares are their preferred prey.

often flicking them as they walk. Their high-rumped, long-legged gait makes it appear as if they are rocking, or "bobbing," when they run. Extremely agile, bobcats can climb trees, run as fast as a coyote, outswim a dog, and leap ten feet or more. Highly intelligent, they are notorious for their ability to outsmart hound dogs by backtracking over their scented trail, leaving the dogs literally barking up the wrong tree.

Bobcats have been called the spitfires of the animal kingdom—fast, fearless, and willing to stand and fight when provoked. Even the kittens have been called "meaner than strychnine." Early settlers who hunted these "wildcats" believed bobcat fur was beneficial when used in poultices to cure wounds. They also thought skin ailments such as pimples, boils, and carbuncles would vanish if certain bobcat body parts were consumed. A more benign legend holds that bobcats ride deer through the woods. Bobcats do kill deer and probably go for a few unexpected rides when they ambush them.

The bobcat's favorite food is rabbit, but it will eat other small animals, such as muskrats, squirrels, snakes, mountain beavers, cotton rats, birds, and fish. During winter it is the smaller prey, such as small birds and voles, that sustain these cats. They also stalk bighorn ewes and lambs, and prey five to ten times their weight—namely deer. These solitary hunters often wait in ambush along game trails and will lie motionless on a rock or log for hours until prey appears. Then, the cat flattens itself, carefully anticipating the moment to spring. Its success or failure depends on the initial attack. Should a large animal be killed, a bobcat will eat its fill, then cover the carcass for later consumption.

During the breeding period early each year, the deep-throated growls, high-pitched squeals, snarls, and hissing calls of the caterwauling males carry for a mile or more. Bobcats also signal to one another using pungent scent marks, their tufted ears, and manxlike tails. Females hold their tails erect as white beacons for their kittens to follow. White rings around the eyes and white markings under the nose help highlight facial expressions. The bobcat's ear tufts are thought to serve as sound-amplifying antennae to help locate prey. In fact, studies have indicated that captive bobcats may lose some of their ability to hear well if the tufts are cut off.

As with the elusive mountain lion, few people ever see the secretive, cryptically-colored bobcat.

In fact, only in 1965, with improvements in both transmitters and receivers, was it first possible to use radio telemetry to make detailed observations of the bobcat in the wild. This technology helped shed light on the ecology and home range patterns of this resilient feline.

The bobcat's relationship to people is an interesting one. While we have eliminated these cats

in many areas of the East and Midwest due to hunting and habitat destruction, in some areas people have actually helped increase bobcat habitat by breaking up forests into rodent-producing fields and woodlots. Bobcats prey on agricultural pests, such as mice, rabbits, and hares. In spite of some livestock killing, bobcats play an important role helping to keep farm areas free of pests.

In the meantime, bobcat skins continue to be in high demand, particularly their spotted belly fur. An estimated ninety thousand bobcat and lynx pelts are traded each year in the world's legal fur markets. With the continuing population declines and increased protection of the tropical cats, the bobcat and North American lynx have become increasingly exploited.

NORTH AMERICAN LYNX

Lynx canadensis

CANADA AND ALASKA

The shy North American lynx (*Lynx canadensis*) is often confused with the bobcat, but is easily outcompeted by this more aggressive, stub-tailed species. With oversized feet that act as snowshoes, lynx are right at home in deep snow. In Greek, the word *lynx* means "to shine," which may refer to the nocturnal eye shine characteristic of all cats.

Along with the cougar and bobcat, the North American lynx is one of the continent's three largest cats. Tufted ears, a stubby four-inch tail, exaggerated cheek fur, and extremely long hind legs give this reclusive feline a distinctive tilted look. Even so, lynx are easily confused with the more aggressive bobcats—they are similar in size and body build, but the bobcat's feet and ear tufts are smaller and its tail is barred. The boundary between their ranges generally follows the U.S.-Canadian border, although a few lynx live in the mountainous states bordering Canada. With long legs and oversized four-inch feet ideal for snowshoeing, lynx are best adapted to the high country of Canada and Alaska, where snow lingers into early summer.

The word "lynx" comes from the Greek word meaning "to shine," which may refer to this cat's highly reflective yellow-green eyes. According to Greek mythology, not only could Lyncaeus see through stone walls, but so could lynx. Described as playful, clever cats with the anatomy of a square, lynx have large, triangular ears tipped with black tufts of hair, and a distinctive ruff of hair around their necks. Their thick, white-tipped fur gives them a frosted look much like the Pallas' cat.

The North American lynx is the smallest of all three species of lynx, and the most indistinctly spotted. Weighing around twenty-two pounds, it looks bigger due to its long legs and thick fur. When summer arrives, lynx shed their heavy

habits have hampered research, they are thought to be common throughout central and southern Africa. Classified as vermin due to their predation on poultry and livestock, caracals have endured expensive extermination campaigns. Yet despite such persecution, the caracal is one of the only species of wild felids that has successfully resisted. Habitat loss has eliminated their natural prey, and natural rivals, the black-backed jackals, while introducing goats and sheep as substitute food.

SERVAL

Felis serval

AFRICA

Servals are shaped like no other cat. They are called the "spare parts" cat, and their long necks, small heads, and oversized, oval ears give these felines a unique appearance. The name "serval" is derived from a Portuguese word meaning "wolf-deer"—an apt description for a graceful carnivore with deerlike long legs and large, rounded ears on a small, slim head. In proportion to the rest of its body, the serval has the longest legs in the felid family—so long that when this thirty-five-pound cat lies down, it keeps its front legs outstretched canine-style. Servals inhabit the grasslands, thorn scrub, and savanna woodlands of Africa from sea level to 10,500 feet. Their beautiful golden fur is marked by black dots and freckles. Black servals also occur.

While hunting in tall grass, servals use their enormous ears to detect the most imperceptible sounds. At night, and in dense grass, they rely on sound alone to locate their prey. Servals feed on hares, guinea fowl, cane rats, mole rats, duikers, lizards, fish—even domestic stock. They can make high leaps to snare low-flying birds, such as a ten-pound guinea fowl, and have been observed killing fifteen-pound Thomson's gazelles.

The serval's long legs are used to make a series of graceful, bounding leaps through tall grass—not to chase down prey. Should a small animal suddenly break cover, this agile, solitary hunter leaps high in the air to dive and pin its prey. Listening to underground movement, these patient predators have been observed sitting beside the entrance to mole rat burrows, waiting to hook and fling their occupants. It has been estimated that a serval eats about 4,000 rodents, 260 snakes, and 130 birds in a year.

Besides man, leopards and dogs are the serval's main predators. Some African tribes consider "steak serval" a delicacy. Others use their pelts to make fur cloaks called *karrosses*. The serval's exotic spots also make it a target for poachers. As part of the illicit trade in cat skins, serval pelts are occasionally marketed as young leopard or cheetah, which are more valuable. Conversion of grasslands to agriculture, and depredation as poultry and sheep pests, continue to reduce the serval's unknown numbers.

With enormous ears, long legs, and a small head, the African serval (*Felis serval*) is as eye-catching as its habit of pouncing on rodents. It is thought that even the dense hair lining the entrance to its ears may function, like whiskers, to detect air currents and vibrations to help locate prey.

ASIAN GOLDEN CAT

Felis temmincki

SOUTHEAST ASIA, NEPAL TO BURMA, CHINA, THAILAND, VIETNAM, PENINSULAR MALAYSIA, AND SUMATRA

Called the fire cat throughout parts of Asia, the Asian golden cat is well known in both myth and legend. According to one tale, if a person carries just a single hair from a golden cat, it will protect the bearer from tigers. To rid an entire village of tigers, a whole pelt must be burned. Some Thai villagers cook the cat, fur and all, believing that when eaten, it will keep all animals from attacking. While these beliefs are tough on the species, they illustrate the significant role these medium-sized cats have played in Asian mythology.

This secretive feline inhabits forest and dense bushland along the southern border of the Himalayas through Southeast Asia. Like its African counterpart, the Asian species comes in a variety of hues, from gold, red, or gray to black, its white belly also marked with spots and stripes or just plain. Slightly larger than the African golden cat, and more abundant, the Asian golden cat is the largest species of the genus *Felis* found in Thailand.

Early observers once mistakenly compared these gold-toned cats with the cougar or puma and called them *catopuma*. Today in parts of China they are called the "rock cat." Nothing is known of their social behavior in the wild. Although their young have been found in the hollows of trees, golden cats are thought to be mostly terrestrial, pursuing a diet of small mammals, birds, reptiles, and poultry on the ground. It has been proposed that the white underside of their tail, held up like a taillight, gives the young a beacon to follow, particularly in the dark.

The forest-dwelling Asian golden cat (*Felis temmincki*), native to Southeast Asia, is larger than its African relative, but can be just as variable in coat color, marked with or without spots and stripes. In pursuit of birds, lizards, and small mammals, it will occasionally kill domestic poultry and livestock.

Persecuted as poultry pests by farmers, these endangered cats are most threatened by continued deforestation. Unlike the adaptable leopard cat, Asian golden cats are intolerant of any human interference.

AFRICAN GOLDEN CAT

Felis aurata

WEST AND CENTRAL AFRICA, PARTS OF UGANDA

Found in the equatorial forests of west and central Africa, the little-known African golden cat is named after its soft, gold-toned fur. This seems straightforward enough, except that golden cats have some of the most variable coat colorings of any felids. Their fur can vary from gray to orange, be plain or spotted, gold or all-black. Their cheeks, chin, and underparts are usually pale in color. Their bellies can be covered in dark spots, or have none at all. Like the Borneo Bay cat, this species has rounded ears with black backsides.

African golden cats are one of the few felid species that inhabit the tropical rain forests of western Africa. They are also found in dense secondary vegetation, alpine moorland, and along waterways that extend into drier, more open habitat. About twice the size of a large house cat, they vary in size depending on geographic region. Active at twilight, these nocturnal hunters pursue rodents, monkeys, birds, and hyraxes. Although they are thought to do most of their hunting on the ground, golden cats are skilled tree climbers and have been observed resting in low tree branches by day.

The global population of African golden cats is thought to be less than 50,000 and decreasing primarily due to loss of its rain forest habitat. Golden cats are also killed for their pelts, for human consumption, and as poultry pests. Very little else is known about these elusive cats in the wild.

Roughly twice the size of a house cat, the African golden cat (*Felis aurata*), native to west and central Africa, has one of the most variable coat colors of any species of wild cat.

LEOPARD CAT

Felis bengalensis

PAKISTAN, INDIA, SOUTHERN HIMALAYAS, BANGLADESH, THAILAND, BURMA, VIETNAM, THE MALAY PENINSULA, INDONESIA, AND PARTS OF MAINLAND CHINA TO EASTERN RUSSIA

The leopard cat (*Felis bengalensis*) is being crossbred with domestic cats to produce a hybrid sold as a "Bengal cat." Not only do such practices dilute this species' gene pool, but they also remove potential breeding cats from much-needed conservation programs.

The small, spotted leopard cat is one of the most common wild cats of southern Asia. About the size of a house cat on long legs, this adaptable feline thrives in a variety of habitats, from dense tropical forests, secondary vegetation, and pine forests to semidesert. Clever and resourceful, and not intolerant of people, leopard cats are often found in search of rodents near villages, where they occasionally raid poultry houses. These agile, tree- and ground-hunting cats are also credited with helping to control rodent populations within palm oil and rubber tree plantations.

Leopard cats are remarkable for their seemingly endless variation in color and pattern. They were first described in 1792 as a yellowish cat with black markings from India, but subsequent explorations through Asia revealed specimens whose background color was pale brown, gray, or rufous, such as the leopard cats from Borneo—all with white underparts. In China, these cats are called *chin-ch'ien mao*, or the "money cat," because their spots are said to look like Chinese coins.

While studying wild cats in Thailand's Huai Kha Khaeng Wildlife Sanctuary, Alan Rabinowitz radio-collared a female and three male leopard cats. He discovered that they were active 50 percent of the time, preferring to rest and move on the ground over territories that ranged from 1.5 to 7.5 square kilometers.

At night, the leopard cats hunt for rodents, lizards, amphibians, and other small mammals, including small deer. It is said that they sometimes ambush their prey from trees and catch birds by dropping on them from above. They also patrol caves to feed on reptiles, fallen bats, and swifts.

Leopard cats are good swimmers. In fact, the type specimen was originally caught swimming in the Bay of Bengal. Many have swum considerable distances to populate the offshore islands of Thailand. Like several species of small wild felids, they build their dens in tree hollows, small caves, or in holes beneath the roots of fallen trees. Two to three young are born following a ten-week gestation period.

As smart and adaptable as this versatile species may be, leopard cats are still getting the squeeze from people. Many end up in stew pots; others are persecuted for the fur trade—leopard cat coats and pelts are sold in gift shops throughout Asia. Domestic cat breeders occasionally cross pure leopard cats with a variety of domestic cats to produce hybrids sold as "Bengal cats." Such tampering further dilutes the species' gene pool.

MARBLED CAT

Felis marmorata

SUMATRA, BORNEO, BURMA, THAILAND, VIETNAM, INDOCHINA, PENINSULAR MALAYSIA, INDIA, NEPAL, ASSAM, AND SIKKIM

Resembling a small clouded leopard, this little-known, arboreal cat lives in the tropical forests of Southeast Asia, where its cryptic coloration helps it blend into the lush vegetation. It is said that the only way to spot this beautiful cat in the wild is to look for its long, fat tail dangling from a branch. The marbled cat is only slightly

The leopard cat (*Felis bengalensis*) enjoys a wide distribution over much of Southeast Asia. However, as with most species of small cats, nothing is known about its social system in the wild.

Comparable in size and habits to the New World arboreal margay, the marbled cat (*Felis marmorata*) of Southeast Asia is equally at home in the trees, where it feeds on squirrels, bats, other rodents, reptiles, and insects.

bigger than a house cat, so its tail does look as if it should be attached to a much larger feline. The long, plump appendage—one of the longest tails relative to body size among the *Felidae*—is an adaptation for life in the trees, helping the cat to balance during its high-wire pursuit of prey. As the result of such niche similarities, the marbled cat has been called the margay of Southeast Asia.

Very little is known about this obscure nocturnal feline. The marbled cat gets its name from the marbled appearance of its thick, soft fur, marked with dark blotches, stripes, and spots. Its legs are covered with black spots, and the back of each ear with a white spot. Although protected in Thailand and India, this cat's population size and reproductive habits remain a mystery. One thing is certain: The marbled cats' dependence on undisturbed tropical rain forests makes them as vulnerable as the remaining forests of Southeast Asia.

FISHING CAT

Felis viverrina

SRI LANKA, SOUTHWEST INDIA, BANGLADESH, VIETNAM, THAILAND, BURMA, CHINA, SUMATRA, AND JAVA

Native to Asia, this scruffy-looking cat defies all legends about cats and water. Unlike the house cat, which balks at a bath and flees from the garden hose, the rare fishing cat is a strong swimmer and willingly leaps into streams and deep pools to catch frogs, crustaceans, and fish. Most at home in wetland habitats, such as marshes, mangrove swamps, and the densely vegetated areas along streams and rivers, this unusual green-eyed cat has no problem getting wet from head to tail.

Well adapted to an aquatic lifestyle, the fishing cat has small, round ears that are set back on its head, and a somewhat elongated muzzle. Its grizzled brown fur is coarse and short, and its tail length is reduced. Its front toes are partially webbed, and even when fully retracted, the front claws still protrude. Weighing about twenty-five pounds, this powerful cat also preys on birds, small mammals, and reptiles, and has been accused of killing calves and dogs.

Fishermen could learn a trick or two by watching the fishing cat in action. When not hidden at rest among the tropical vegetation, fishing cats sit patiently at the edge of a stream watching the water. Should a school of fish swim within range, the cat strikes like lightning to bat one onto shore. At other times, this water-loving cat can be seen standing belly deep in a quiet pool, staring intently into the water. Passing fish are grabbed with both paws and quickly brought to the mouth for a lethal bite.

In the wild, fishing cats utilize tree hollows and dense shrubbery to construct their dens. Two to three young are born after a nine-week gestation period. Almost nothing is known about the social behavior of fishing cats in the wild. There are unverified reports that males of the species help care for their young. The observance of several fishing cats together in the wild suggests a sociability rare among wild felids. Even in captivity they show great tolerance for one another, making it possible to house several adults in the same enclosure.

Fishing cats have been hunted for their pelts, eliminated as barnyard pests—and eaten. The cat's flesh is considered edible in many parts of Asia. However, loss of wetlands puts this feline at greatest risk. Development of mangrove and freshwater swamps and deforestation of riverine habitats eliminates the real estate needed by fishing cats.

A pair of fishing cats (*Felis viverrina*) search a stream for aquatic prey. With a somewhat discontinuous distribution throughout Southeast Asia, this unique water-loving cat proves that members of the family *Felidae* have filled just about every available niche.

FLAT-HEADED CAT

The odd-looking flat-headed cat (*Felis planiceps*), native to peninsular Malaysia and Indonesia, has big eyes and ears that ride low on the sides of the head. Named for its long, sloping forehead, this little-known species, like the fishing cat, is thought to eat fish and frogs along riverbanks, as well as rodents.

Felis planiceps

INDONESIA, BORNEO, THAILAND, AND PENINSULAR MALAYSIA

This civet look-alike seems more viverrid than cat. Named for its long, narrow head and flattened forehead, the flat-headed cat is one of the most unusual of felines. Small, rounded ears spaced far apart on the sides of the head and large eyes placed close together help exaggerate the flattened effect. This four- to five-pound felid can be found along the forested riverbanks and waterways of tropical Southeast Asia, where it hunts for frogs and fish at night.

Part of the odd appearance of these cats is due to the many adaptations they have for a semi-aquatic lifestyle, including a short, thickly furred tail, short legs, and feet with long, narrow pads, over which protrude only partially retractile claws. The position of their eyes over an elongated snout maximizes binocular vision needed for fishing. Even their dentition has been modified: Their elongated jaws hold sharp, backward-facing teeth and modified first premolars ideal for seizing slippery prey.

Flat-headed cats enter water freely, dive well, and routinely submerge their heads underwater to catch prey. In captivity they have been observed playing in a tub of water for hours, and washing their food much like a raccoon. As a result, the flat-headed cat has been called the ecological equivalent of a semi-aquatic mustelid.

As is true for most small, wild felids, nothing is known about the flat-headed cat's reproductive behavior or ecology in the wild. In fact, they were teetering toward extinction in 1985 until a few were subsequently found preying on rodents in Malaysia's palm oil plantations. Development of plantations seems to have benefited the species with an increase in rodents. Otherwise, deforestation and illegal live capture for trade and human consumption continue to threaten the future of this secretive little cat.

RUSTY-SPOTTED CAT

Felis rubiginosa

SRI LANKA, SOUTHERN INDIA, AND JAMMU/GUJARAT IN NORTHERN INDIA

This tiny, nocturnal felid with large amber eyes is much smaller than a house cat. Weighing little more than two pounds, the rusty-spotted cat beats the black-footed cat, oncilla, and kodkod as the smallest wild cat in the world. Because of its size and active behavior, it has been called the hummingbird of cat species. It stands just seven inches high and is covered with rich russet-brown fur marked with darker spots.

In Sri Lanka, these petite cats can be found from sea level along the arid coastline to humid forest and low scrub at nearly seven thousand feet. In southern India, they show a similar diver-

sity of habitats, from grasslands to moist deciduous forest. Because of their agile climbing skills in captivity, rusty-spotted cats are thought to spend part of their time hunting birds, small mammals, reptiles, and insects in trees. In India they have been found in the roofs of huts. A rusty-spotted cat kept as a pet by the nineteenth-century naturalist T. C. Jerdon hunted tree squirrels in the rafters of his house. They have also been found living in abandoned houses in southern India far from the forest, sustained on an urban diet of rats, mice, and poultry.

Adults have been mistaken for baby leopards and destroyed when the tiny cat's ferocious personality is unleashed in self-defense. In Sri Lanka, where they are considered edible, the little cats are easily caught with nets, using the paralyzing beam of a flashlight to blind them when they come out to feed on rodents and frogs after a heavy rain. Cooking pots aside, rusty-spotted cats are most vulnerable to habitat destruction.

IRIOMOTE CAT

Felis iriomotensis

IRIOMOTE ISLAND NEAR TAIWAN

Resembling the fishing and leopard cats of Asia, the rare, little-known Iriomote cat was discovered in 1965 by Japanese naturalist Yukio Togawa. Named after the remote Japanese island on which it lives, this small cat was the second new felid species to be found in a century. Initial reports announced that the Iriomote *yamaneko* was a living fossil which had existed for at least three million years.

Iriomote Island is one of the Yaeyama islands, the southernmost group in Japan's Ryukyu island chain. The Yaeyama islands have been called the "Galapagos of the Orient" due to the incredible number of birds, plants, and butterflies that inhabit them. Located at the southern-

This demure, two-pound cat is considered the world's smallest species of wild feline. Less than half the size of a small house cat, the rusty-spotted cat (*Felis rubiginosa*) inhabits humid forests and scrub primarily in southern India and Sri Lanka, ranging from sea level to seven thousand feet, in search of small prey.

reflected a partially arboreal lifestyle (*Animal Kingdom,* November/December 1988).

Iriomote cats have two breeding seasons each year, from February to March and from September to October. Up to four kittens are born, following a two-month gestation period. Dens have been located in the hollows of trees located six feet off the ground. White ear spots and white markings that encircle the eyes and run from the forehead down to the nose help these night-active cats communicate in the dark.

At one time eaten as a delicacy, the rare Iriomote cat is now fully protected. However, their status is considered critical because fewer than one hundred are thought to remain in the wild. Accidental trapping, competition with domestic cats, and the potential for disease transference from domestic cats continue to put them at risk. To help safeguard these vulnerable felines, the Japanese government set aside a third of the island as a national park and in 1972 designated the Iriomote *yamaneko* an official "national treasure," which bans all trapping. Yet island residents have resisted heftier conservation measures in favor of continued economic development. A proposed dam, new roads, and construction of an airport on the nearby island of Ishigaki may further threaten this ancient cat.

BORNEAN BAY CAT

Felis badia

BORNEO

The least known of all Asian felids, the bay cat of Borneo continues to elude description. There are no detailed observations of live animals of this species, and no studies have been conducted in the wild. Nothing is known about its habits, ecology, social behavior, or reproductive biology. All information about this phantom, chestnut-colored cat has been gleaned from six skins as well as a museum specimen collected in 1874.

Based on size and coloration, this mysterious cat appears most closely related to the Asian golden cat, of which it may be a subspecies. These pale-bellied cats are thought to eat rainforest birds, small mammals, monkeys, and carrion. Due to the paucity of information about this felid, and the difficulty of observing them in

Found only on Iriomote Island, a 113-square-mile island located off the east coast of Taiwan, the rare Iriomote cat (*Felis iriomotensis*) is endangered due to its restricted range and interbreeding with feral domestic cats. This feline was first discovered in 1965, and subsequently declared a national treasure by the government of Japan, but fewer than one hundred Iriomote cats are thought to survive. (*Painting by Art Wolfe*)

most tip of this Japanese archipelago, just 120 miles east of Taiwan, Iriomote Island is one of the last patches of wilderness left in Japan. The hilly, forested, 113-square-mile island is covered by broadleaf evergreen forests and has estuaries lined with dense mangroves—the northernmost limit of mangrove forests in Asia.

It is here that the secretive, nocturnal, little-known Iriomote cat prowls the beaches, forests, and trees for prey. About the size of a domestic cat, this bespotted, amber-eyed feline eats everything from large skinks, fruit bats, birds, and snakes to insects, crabs, and fish. As with all cats, a reduction in premolars and molars has led to a shortening of the Iriomote cat's jaw, a less protuberant muzzle, and the rounded appearance of its head. In the Iriomote cat, the first premolar is absent. Shigeki Yasuma, who studied this species in the wild, discovered that they do not usually hold their prey with their forepaws or loosen their bite while attacking, adaptations he felt the wild, the Borneo bay cat has been listed as endangered. Continued loss of habitat due to logging and human encroachment poses the greatest threat to its survival—and our chances of ever learning more about this elusive feline.

OCELOT

Felis pardalis

SOUTHERN TEXAS, PARTS OF MEXICO, CENTRAL AMERICA THROUGH SOUTH AMERICA TO ARGENTINA

Walking along a dirt road in the middle of Belize's Cockscomb Basin Jaguar Preserve, I had the rare opportunity to see an ocelot in the wild. From a distance, in the early morning light, it appeared bigger than any I had ever seen in captivity. With wild-cat elegance, the graceful feline quietly walked along the edge of the dirt road. Its magnificent spotted coat, seen against the rain-forest backdrop, enhanced the exotic encounter. When it finally turned its head to make brief eye contact, the dignified cat did not run, but continued unintimidated, calmly walking off the road to disappear into the vegetation.

Ocelots are one of the best known of the small *Felidae,* thanks in part to the fur industry, and trade in exotic pets. Similar in appearance to the margay, ocelots are much larger, weighing twenty to thirty pounds or more. To the confusion of early taxonomists, they show great regional and individual variability in coat color. Their short fur is marked with black-rimmed blotches and spots in designs as unique as a fingerprint. Sleeping by day and hunting at night, these adaptable cats inhabit dry deciduous forests, dry scrub, seasonally flooded savannas, and tropical rain forests. Concealed by spots and darkness, an ocelot becomes almost invisible during its mostly terrestrial search for food—a bird, rodent, snake, or lizard. Come dawn, this spotted cat returns to the treetops to snooze away the day safely camouflaged among the leaves.

Called *maracaja* in Brazil, in reference to their spots, ocelots once ranged from the southwestern United States through Mexico, Central and South America to Argentina. Coveted for their beautiful spotted fur, ocelots have been decimated throughout their historic range.

According to Paul Leyhausen, every ocelot coat takes at least one dozen adult skins to make. If just three of those animals include lactating females, then an additional three to six ocelots are lost. Statistics such as these, coupled with habitat loss, explain why ocelots are now listed as endangered and vulnerable throughout most of their remaining range. Only about a hundred are left in the southern tip of Texas. The rest survive in the most remote jungles and protected reserves of Central and South America.

Since 1981 wildlife specialist Michael Tewes has conducted a long-term study of ocelots at the Laguna Atascosa National Wildlife Refuge in southern Texas (*National Wildlife,* June/July 1994). His study subjects, radio-collared and DNA-fingerprinted, have revealed a preference for the densest tracts of mesquite, thorny underbrush, and ebony. Such habitat offers not only an abundance of cottontails, field mice, and birds, but protection from natural enemies, such as wild dogs, coyotes, and people. However, in

Almost nothing is known about the bay cat, or Bornean red cat (*Felis badia*), other than that it exists only on the island of Borneo. The little that is known has been gleaned from six museum skins and a single specimen collected in 1874. (*Painting by Art Wolfe*)

well known for her ability to breed, and if necessary hand-raise, small wild cats in captivity. During her nearly three decades managing tigrinas, she once observed the unusual teething pattern of a twenty-one-day-old kitten. After the cat had shown no signs of any teeth, all age-appropriate teeth suddenly erupted within a matter of hours.

Generally, says Quillen, the smaller the cat, the more hyperactive and alert it is. Felid specialist Paul Leyhausen once observed an oncilla kill a brown rat after a difficult fight. Typical of felid play behavior, the cat vigorously flung, chased, sprang on, pawed, and kicked at the dead rat for half an hour afterward.

According to ecologist Norman Myers (*International Wildlife*, March/April 1976), small felids exhibit more stealth, cunning, and ferocity than big cats, with hair-trigger temperaments and restless energy. Lacking the stamina for an extended chase, small cats usually seize their prey within a stride or two—or move on. They depend on concealment by camouflage and inconspicuous movement.

A decade ago oncillas were heavily hunted for their exotic fur, along with margays, ocelots, and Geoffroy's cats. Deforestation and poaching continue to threaten the survival of this small, endangered cat.

GEOFFROY'S CAT

Felis geoffroyi

PARTS OF BRAZIL, PARAGUAY, URUGUAY, CHILE, AND THE BOLIVIAN ANDES AND MOUNTAINS OF NORTHWEST ARGENTINA

When field biologists first took a casual look at the Geoffroy's cat, they could not find any trace of their scats—the stock and trade of feline research. It took a while to figure out that this small, partly arboreal cat defecates in trees, often over water, rarely leaving a trace of its eating habits on the ground. This versatile cat can be found in open bush, rocky terrain, scrub woodlands, and riverine forest. It hunts for rodents, reptiles, birds, and insects on the ground as well as in trees, from where it is said to drop from low branches onto its prey. Active

at night, this house cat–sized felid often sleeps in trees by day.

Named after the French naturalist Geoffroy St. Hilaire, this small-spotted cat looks like a larger version of an oncilla. Its coat color varies from black to silvery gray or bright ochre depending on geographic location. The darker, more melanistic forms occur in the heavily forested areas of the cat's range, while the largest specimens are found in their southern range. While hunting, the female leaves her young in a camouflaged nest made of leaves and debris. In captivity, Pat Quillen observed a female pull her kittens up onto her feet and wrap her tail around

Another victim of the illegal trade in spotted furs, the tabby-sized Geoffroy's cat (*Felis geoffroyi*) has an attractive coat of spots that can range in hue from silver to auburn—even jet black. This swimming, climbing rodent hunter inhabits riverine forests and scrublands from the Bolivian Andes south through Chile.

Right: This silver-colored pampas cat (*Felis colocolo*) has auburn stripes on its legs. Aside from the knowledge that pampas cats come in various hues, nothing is known about their social or reproductive behavior in the wild.

Below: Since it's about the same size as a house cat, only the pointed ears, fat cheeks, and coarse hair give this creature away as a melanistic form of pampas cat (*Felis colocolo*).

them in cool weather. Geoffroy's cats are found at elevations from sea level to nine thousand feet. In fact, their local name, *gato montes,* means "mountain cat." In northern Argentina, where their spotted pattern is indistinct, this subspecies is called the "salt desert cat."

The Geoffroy's relationship to people runs the full gamut: they are eaten, kept as pets, used for rodent control, and shot as poultry pests. Domestic cat breeders have begun to cross pure specimens with a variety of domestic cats to produce a gene-diluting hybrid called the "safari cat." However, it is the species' spots that are causing the biggest problem. Having decimated the ocelot and margay populations, hunters are now going after Geoffroy's cat pelts using guns, traditional traps, and lures that mimic the enticing sound of their distressed prey. While it takes three jaguar skins or twelve ocelot skins to make a long fur coat, it takes twenty Geoffroy's cat pelts to do the same—an inexcusably high price for fashion.

PAMPAS CAT

Felis colocolo

Parts of Ecuador, Peru, Chile, Argentina, Uruguay, Paraguay, and Brazil

The broad-faced pampas cat has one of the most intriguing faces in the feline family. It is reminiscent of the face masks used in the Broadway hit *Cats*. Named after the treeless South American plains, or pampas, where it lives, the pampas cat is another Neotropical feline of which very little is known. Its Latin name apparently honors the renowned Araucanian warrior chief Colocolo.

Slightly bigger than a domestic cat, but more robustly built, with a longer head and tail, this leg-barred cat has the most pointed ears of any South American felid. It also occurs in the most remarkable color patterns, from all black to silver-gray, red, or gold, with rufous spots and bands, yellow or black bands, or no pattern at all. In addition, these cats have a distinctive mane of hair along their backs which can be raised to signal fear or aggression.

Pampas cats occur in a variety of habitats, including humid forests and high-altitude cloud forests. In Argentina, they are called *gato pajero*, the "grass cat," due to their association with the high *pajero* grass of the open plains. Typical of many small felid species, pampas cats frequent border zones between two environments, in this case the area where forest gives way to grasslands. Here they can exploit prey from two ecological habitats. It is assumed that they are nocturnal, feeding on rodents and ground-nesting birds. They occasionally raid henhouses. Very little else is known about their behavior in the wild.

ANDEAN MOUNTAIN CAT

Felis jacobita

High Andes of Peru, Bolivia, Chile, and Argentina

The rare, little-known Andean mountain cat is yet another species of felid ghost. Although this cat was first described to science in 1865, it was

Pampas cats come in a variety of color patterns depending on their geographic location in South America. This Brazilian pampas cat (*Felis colocolo*) has a larger nose and coarse reddish fur highlighted with distinctive black leg bands.

Weighing little more than five pounds, with a short, ringed tail, the rare kodkod (*Felis guigna*) rivals the oncilla as the smallest wild cat in South America. Restricted to a forested area in Chile and Argentina, this species is particularly sensitive to habitat destruction.

not until 1980 that a positive sighting was made. The only information available on the behavior of this species comes from those two hours of observation, a few photographs, and specimen skins.

Like the Pallas' cat and snow leopard from the Himalayas, this eight-pound cat is well adapted to life at high altitudes. Its thick silver-gray fur, marked with dark brown spots and stripes, provides protection from the cold and camouflage against the rocky, treeless zone it frequents in the high Andes. Its black-tipped tail, ringed with dark bands, is long and thickly furred.

Their thin-air habitat of cold and perpetual wind is so isolated and rugged that few Andean mountain cats are ever seen. Only a few have been collected in the wild, most at elevations

approaching ten thousand feet. This speaks as much to their ability to hide among the rocks and vegetation as to their scarcity. The stuffed specimen of this rare little cat is stored in the archives of the Natural History Museum of London.

KODKOD

Felis guigna

RESTRICTED RANGE IN CHILE AND ARGENTINA

This shy little cat rivals the oncilla as the smallest cat in the Western Hemisphere. It is extremely rare in the wild, and its geographic range is

near human habitation. In Egypt it is called the "reed" or "swamp" cat. This lithe, long-limbed feline is a terrestrial hunter that runs down its prey, feeding on a diet as varied as its habitat. It eats rodents, lizards, frogs, and fish, along with insects and deer fawns—even poultry. Like caracals, jungle cats can make high vertical leaps to capture birds. They also eat carrion and meat scraps left behind at tiger kills.

Depending on their geographic location, jungle cats can weigh anywhere from ten to thirty-five pounds. They tend to be larger farther north in their range—the biggest cats are found in Soviet Central Asia. Their plain, unspotted coat can be brown, gray, or reddish. All-black jungle cats occur in India and Pakistan. Their long-legged, elongated body and narrow face, with high, pointed ears tipped with black hair tufts, give these mono-colored cats a sphinxlike appearance. The ancient Egyptians once depicted jungle cats in wall paintings and mummified them along with African wildcats and domestic cats for placement in their tombs. Because of this and anatomical similarities, the jungle cat is associated with the lineage of the domestic cat.

Although the jungle cat's plain-colored coat is not a coveted pelt, these cats are eliminated as poultry pests, and by sportsmen who claim the cats kill game species such as hares and francolins. Jungle cats breed easily with domestic cats, producing hybrids. Typical of a tenacious survivor, this species breeds well under adverse conditions.

PALLAS' CAT

Felis manul

FROM THE CASPIAN SEA AND IRAN TO CHINA AND SOUTHEAST SIBERIA

The flat-faced, short-legged Pallas' cat definitely looks like a cat with an attitude. With ears positioned on the sides of its head, a squashed face, polka-dot forehead, and glowering eyes, it looks like the Cheshire cat on a bad day. Most of this "don't mess with me" appearance has to do with the Pallas' cat's physical adaptations to a high-altitude environment—the inhospitable steppes, cold deserts, and treeless, rocky mountainsides of central Asia. Found as high as thirteen thousand feet, the Pallas' cat is able to tolerate extremes of

heat and cold with feet that are furred for protection from hot sand and freezing snow, long belly fur for insulation, and a thick fur-muff tail that can be wrapped around its feet. In fact, the Pallas' cat holds title as being covered by the longest, densest fur of any wild cat in the world. Weighing only about six pounds, this feisty feline looks bigger and heavier than it actually is, due to its thick reddish-gray fur. White-tipped hairs enhance the effect by making the fur look frosted.

Named after German naturalist Peter Pallas, who described much of Russia's wildlife, the Pallas' cat uses caves, rocks, and crevices for cover. Its sideways ears, broad, flattened head, and wide-spaced yellow eyes enable it to peer over the tops of rocks without being detected by predator or prey. It feeds on birds and small mammals, such as pikas, marmots, hares, and ground squirrels. With no trees for escape from predators, this pugnacious cat has learned how to hold its own. Since it lives under such extreme conditions, with hunters after its luxurious pelt, it is no wonder this cat looks tough.

CHINESE DESERT CAT

Felis bieti

China: eastern Tibetan plateau north to Inner Mongolia

Covered with long, dense yellowish-gray fur, the Chinese desert cat is another small felid about which virtually nothing is known. For starters, its name is misleading, as these slightly tuft-eared cats live at altitudes up to nine thousand feet, in steppes and woodland forests—not deserts. In fact, a more appropriate name might be the Chinese mountain cat. Bigger than a domestic cat, this elusive carnivore frequents the same habitat used by the golden snub-nosed monkey and the giant panda. It has been suggested that this enigmatic cat may be a larger subspecies of the wildcat *Felis silvestris.*

Nothing is known about its diet, reproduction, or social system. As with the black-footed cat and sand cat, its feet reflect a harsh terrain. They are protected by tufts of hair growing between the pads. Unfortunately, the best place to see one of these beautiful ring-tailed cats is not in the wilds of the eastern Tibetan plateau, but at a local Szechuan market, where their pelts are occasionally sold.

BLACK-FOOTED CAT

Felis nigripes

Arid areas of South Africa, Botswana, and Namibia

The smallest cat in Africa, and one of the smallest in the world, the feisty black-footed cat inhabits the arid areas of southern Africa. Nicknamed the "tiger of the termite mound"—more for its association with these towering landforms than the folktale that says it can kill a giraffe—this four-pound spitfire can flatten its ears and be as aggressive as a big cat when threatened. It is especially skilled at the neck-aimed kill bite. Yet, since it is half the size of a domestic cat, it would take nearly two hundred black-footed cats to weigh as much as a big Siberian tiger—the world's largest cat.

Weighing little more than four pounds, the black-footed cat (*Felis nigripes*), native to the arid regions of southern Africa, is the smallest species of wild cat on the continent. Named for its black footpads, this diminutive feline is a skilled digger capable of producing a variety of unique vocalizations, from an ear-twitching jaw chatter to a loud meow.

Named for the jet-black pads on their feet, these rare, miniature carnivores are beautifully adapted to life in the desert. To avoid the heat, they hunt at night and rest by day in abandoned aardvark burrows and termite mounds. Black hair on the bottom of their feet helps protect them from the hot, burning sand. They can survive without water for long periods by getting enough moisture from their diet of rodents, spiders, and insects. Their digging skills suggest that they easily pursue small animals that hide in the sand. Food scarcity and susceptibility to predation seem to have shortened their mating period and accelerated the development of their young.

Unlike other feline mothers, female black-footed cats produce a special vocalization that tells the young to scatter and freeze when danger is near. This behavior, seen also in gulls, increases the odds that at least one kitten will survive if the family is attacked. Only when the female gives an almost noiseless chittering "ah-ah-ah" sound, accompanied by synchronous up-and-down movements of her twittering, half-flattened ears, do the kittens regroup around her. Listed as endangered, black-footed cats are fully protected in Africa.

SAND CAT

Felis margarita

NORTHERN SAHARA, EGYPT, ISRAEL, ARABIA, TURKMEN, AND PAKISTAN TO IRAN

With fur the color of its shifting sand-dune habitat, the big-eared, five-pound sand cat is a tough little feline. Native to the shimmering deserts and stony plains of Africa, Asia, and parts of the Middle East, this small cat is built to survive. Its large, silky ears, each marked with a black spot, help detect the faintest sounds of prey and serve as heat dumps, allowing the maximum loss of body heat through the thin skin. Set low on the sides of the head, the ear position helps sand cats remain hidden while peeking over rocks in pursuit of prey. Sand cats eat everything from jerboas, sand voles, hares, and birds to reptiles and insects. Moisture from their prey enables them to live in arid habitats devoid of freestanding water.

Sand cats avoid the heat of day by resting in holes dug under rocks and bushes. Its pale coloration helps keep this cat cool and well camouflaged—so well, in fact, that it is easy to miss seeing these cats even in captivity. Thick fur on the bottoms of their feet act like sandshoes to traverse the hot desert. Often mistaken for barking dogs at night, sand cats produce a similar vocalization that has been described as both yodeling and barking. These loud calls carry over the desert, enabling the solitary cats to find a mate when needed.

DOMESTIC CAT

Felis sylvestris catus

WORLDWIDE

It is now generally agreed that domestication of the African wildcat (*Felis sylvestris lybica*), begun in Egypt about four thousand years ago, led to the dozing felines we now have curled up on our hearths. Since then, more than forty different breeds totaling more than 100 million domestic cats have dispersed around the globe. *Felis s. catus* has become one of the most popular pets in history. Basically solitary like most felid carnivores, these cats can develop a hierarchical social organization, and appear to tolerate one another in great densities, if given a constant, reliable source of food.

Above: It is now believed that the domestic cat descended from the African wildcat, to which this Arabian desert cat (*Felis silvestris gordoni*) is a close relative.

Opposite: With big, low-slung ears on oversized faces, sand cats (*Felis margarita*) appear top-heavy, with heads too big for their small bodies. Yet these features are part of their adaptation for life in the harsh rock-and-sand-dune deserts of northern Africa and the Middle East, where their ears are used to detect prey, and thick foot pads enable them to walk across the hot sands at night.

5

Living with Wild Cats

PUTTING THE SQUEEZE ON FELINES

Cats are secretive, and it is quite in keeping with their lifelong dignity that they face their end without tears or to-do.

—ROGER CARAS, *A Celebration of Cats*, 1986

According to Zero Population Growth in Washington, D.C., in the seconds it takes you to read this sentence, 24 people will be added to the Earth's population. Every hour 11,000 people are born, every day 260,000. While it took 4 million years to produce 2 billion people, it will only take another thirty years to add another billion. The world population is increasing by 95 million people every year. By the year 2050, the United Nations estimates that 10 billion people will crowd planet Earth.

These numbers foretell global problems for people as well as wildlife. While about 1.4 million species have already been identified, an estimated 10 to 80 million more remain biological mysteries awaiting discovery. As many as fifty to one hundred new species may inhabit a single acre of tropical rain forest, yet these valuable laboratories of plant and animal evolution are being felled at the rate of 4 million acres a year. As more and more land is exploited to meet the economic needs of ravaging human populations, less and less room will be left for the world's wild critters—including the cats. Eventually, we will all face a habitat squeeze.

"The most important goal for the twenty-first century is family planning for everyone," said U.S. Congresswoman Patricia Schroeder (*Time*, Special Issue, "Beyond the Year 2000," Fall 1992). "That is *the* environmental issue. You can plant a billion trees and clean up every stream, but it won't make a difference if we double the population in the next twenty years."

"Habitat loss across the board is the real problem in species survival," says Craig Reiben, spokesperson for the U.S. Fish and Wildlife Service. "Controlling development and habitat degradation before a species is in trouble is the key."

Take, for example, the lion, Africa's largest carnivore. According to ecologist Norman Myers (*International Wildlife*, May/June 1984), "With wildlands shrinking and prey stocks declining in modern Africa, the lion is turning more and more to the next best food—cattle and other domestic stock. Upshot: conflict with people."

Worldwide, an estimated 10 to 15 billion domestic animals—more than a billion of

Above: The shy, solitary snow leopard (*Panthera uncia*) is endangered throughout its range, due to habitat and prey loss, elimination as a livestock pest, and continued poaching for its luxurious spotted fur.

Opposite: Named after its unusual coat pattern, the clouded leopard (*Neofelis nebulosa*) is a skilled tree climber that often drops out of the branches onto its prey. The illegal fur trade, coupled with habitat loss, has put this species at risk.

them ruminants—have taken over habitat once used by wildlife. The ruminants graze over 7 billion acres of land, a mega-pasture equivalent in size to the continental landmass of Africa. Such animal husbandry combined with the farming and firewood collecting needed to sustain burgeoning human populations does not bode well for wildlife or wild habitats. In Africa, lions, leopards, and cheetahs are being killed by

livestock owners due to their loss of animals.

"Industrialized nations can show from their own experience that development itself is ultimately threatened by continued destruction of the ecosystem," wrote Steven Graham (*Sierra*, September/October 1986).

According to Edward O. Wilson in his book *The Diversity of Life* (1992), all environmental problems can be classified into two major

Peruvian farmer clearing rain forest to feed his family. "Progressing from patch to patch as the soil is drained of nutrients, he will cut more kinds of trees than are native to all of Europe. If there is no other way for him to make a living, the trees will fall."

Norman Myers agrees. He feels the proportionate number of Africans becoming educated about the aesthetic value in their wildlife is not keeping up with the overall population growth. "The main problem does not lie with a few thousand poachers with their poisoned arrows," he wrote (*International Wildlife*, March/April 1982), "it lies with many millions of people with their digging hoes. When a farmer is without land and sees his family without food, the most sophisticated sense of aesthetic pleasure gives way to practical considerations."

According to Wilson, the much needed "New Environmentalists" are those people who understand this economic reality. "Only by developing new methods of drawing income from land already cleared, or from intact wildlands themselves," said Wilson, "will biodiversity be saved from the mill of human poverty."

Wild cats and other large predators serve as indicator species measuring the overall health of an ecosystem. The degree of disturbance to natural systems is marked by their presence—or absence. Because felids are the most specialized group of predators, like sensitive barometers, they are the most dramatically affected by any disturbance to biological communities.

For example, increased access to wilderness areas in British Columbia, due to extensive logging coupled with increasing human populations, has made it possible to hunt cougars in virtually all of their available habitat. Such habitat degradation has also reduced the cougars' prey base.

In Africa most species of large mammals are under siege, as are those in Asia, due to habitat loss and human population growth. In Latin America the trend is toward deforestation and the replacement of ecologically more productive, diversified trees with fast-producing timber species. Shrub areas are also being converted to grasslands for livestock.

"Few, if any, areas are free from some form of human disturbance, which can impinge on the lives of wild cats," wrote IUCN Cat Specialist Chair Peter Jackson (*Felid Action Plan*, 1991/1992). "The rate of loss of tropical

Opposite: A clear-cut forest in the Sabah region of Borneo shows why many species of wild cats are now endangered. Habitat loss eliminates both the prey and adequate living space needed for the cats to survive.

groups. The first is alteration of the physical environment through toxic pollution, depletion of arable land and aquifers, loss of the ozone layer, and global warming to a state uncongenial to life. Accelerated human population growth will accomplish this unless trends are voluntarily reduced.

Wilson's second category is the loss of biological diversity. As an example, he describes a forests, home for about two-thirds of the cats, has increased markedly." According to Jackson, India and Thailand, rich in cat species, have lost virtually all of their lowland forests.

"Deforestation has many interwoven consequences," wrote Professors Robert Hazen and James Trefil in their book *Science Matters: Achieving Scientific Literacy* (1991). "As trees are burned, unique habitats are lost, carbon dioxide is added to the atmosphere, oxygen-producing trees are lost, soil erosion is increased, rivers become polluted with mud and silt and delicate river ecosystems are also destroyed." Such ecological losses threaten people as well as wildlife.

"Throughout the Americas, great changes fueled by visions of progress have swept away the habitats of countless plants and animals," reported Alan Weisman and Sandy Tolan (*Audubon,* November/December 1992) after a two-year, fifteen-country study of indigenous people. "But entire human cultures are also becoming endangered."

Historically, Western culture has viewed the lands inhabited by native peoples as reservoirs of marketable resources. Indigenous people were typically exploited—more often eliminated—during utilization of those resources. As Weisman and Tolan point out, "what we do to the lives and lands of others may ultimately determine the fate of our own."

Bernard Nietschmann, a geography professor at the University of California, Berkeley, has studied the Miskito Nation of eastern Nicaragua for the past two decades. He believes their homeland is one of the richest and least disturbed areas remaining in all of Indian Latin America.

"Where there are indigenous populations with a homeland," says Nietschmann, who estimates that five thousand such nations exist in the world, "there are biologically rich environments. Native people protect their homeland because they are bound to it" (*Audubon,* November/December 1992).

For example, most hunter-gatherer societies, such as the Bushmen of the Kalahari, lived in perfect harmony with nature, following ancient ways that protected their natural resources. As with wildlife populations, the size of a Bushman band was limited to the number of people a territory could support without straining the ecosystem. So skilled were they at tapping and

managing their replenishable resources—with extensive knowledge of about two hundred species of plants—that Bushman bands could live in areas of the central Kalahari where there is no water for three hundred days a year. They survived on the juice from wild fruits and tubers, and the fluids squeezed from the rumen of prey animals.

According to South African writer Alf Wannenburgh, who lived with the Bushmen for several months, "They speak of their origins, not in terms of historical tradition, but in reference to a mythical time when all animals were people like themselves, speaking the same language" (*International Wildlife,* March/April 1982).

After joining a Bushman hunting party that used poisoned darts to kill a giraffe, Wannenburgh described how the men could interpret every mark left in the sand by their quarry, and even seemed to anticipate its moves. "Yet, for all their remarkable efficiency at hunting, they followed a strict code," he wrote. "Since animals were once 'people,' the Bushmen believed it was natural to kill for food and in

self-defense, but they considered wanton slaughter a taboo."

Unfortunately, of the thirty thousand or more Bushmen that now survive, only a handful continue to follow their old ways—in the most inpenetrable areas of the Kalahari, where lack of surface water has kept other people at bay. Under the influence of encroaching cultures, many Bushman bands have lost their land, and many have abandoned their traditional ways to become farmers. "The ancient bond between the Bushmen and the land has now all but disap-

peared," said Wannenburgh, "and with it the mutually preserving relationship between hunter and prey."

"If you are interested in cultural diversity, you have to be interested in biological diversity, because nature is the scaffolding of culture," says Nietschmann. "Systems that *do* work are being destroyed to prolong systems that *don't* work."

"The more we learn [about nature]," adds Lewis Thomas (*Audubon*, March/April 1992), "the more we seem to distance ourselves from the rest of life, as though we were separate creatures, so different from other occupants of the biosphere as to have arrived from another galaxy. We seek too much to explain, we assert a duty to run the place, to dominate the planet, to govern its life, but at the same time we ourselves seem to be less a part of it than ever before."

During their travels through the Americas, Weisman and Tolan had a prophetic meeting with an old shaman from the endangered Guarani people of Argentina. These people once inhabited the vast forests from Argentina to the Amazon, but now just a few Indians remain.

"The white man hasn't triumphed," warned the shaman. "When the Indians vanish, the rest will follow."

AN ANIMAL WITHOUT A TERRITORY

The Kamba tribe of East Africa tell a folktale about a farmer who once owned a piece of land far from his house (*Swara*, 1979). When the rains came, he planted seeds. Soon a crop sprouted and grew. This attracted squirrels, who ate the plants, and other animals as well. So the farmer set traps around his field. One day when he checked the traps, he found he had caught a lion who had entered the field to catch the other animals. The lion promised not to return to the field if the man would let him free. But the lion suddenly sprang free and chased the man. The man now promised to give the lion the heart of every animal caught in his traps if he would let him free.

One day, the man's wife went to check the field, and while doing so, got caught in a trap. When his wife didn't return, the man went to the field and discovered what had happened to her. Just as he was about to set her free, the lion suddenly appeared and reminded the man of his promise, threatening to kill both of them if he didn't comply. The man yelled for help at the top of his lungs, but the lion still grabbed his wife, killed her, and ran away with her. The man rushed home to tell his neighbors what

Opposite: An ocelot kitten (*Felis pardalis*) displays the beautiful spotted coat that both camouflages it amid tropical vegetation and makes it a target for the black market trade in spotted furs.

of the populated area, the Washington State Department of Wildlife brought in bloodhounds to help track the cat. If caught, it would be sedated and relocated to a watershed or mountain area away from people. As it turned out, after several weeks of evasion, the 120-pound cat finally wandered into a subdivision of expensive homes—and was killed before a veterinarian could arrive with a tranquilizer gun.

In 1992 cougars killed people in California, Colorado, and British Columbia. They also attacked a small girl near Lake Wenatchee in Washington. More recently, a cougar mauled a two-year-old boy near Enumclaw, Washington. While drought is partly to blame for the increase in cougar encounters, the main reason remains perpetual habitat loss. Such wildlife encounters will only increase as wild animals are squeezed out of living space into remnant patches of habitat.

"One might recall," wrote Norman Myers (*The World's Cats*, 1976), "that there have been enough instances of island populations going wrong, islands ecological as well as geographical."

SPORT HUNTING

To Kill a Rival Predator

When man kills the natural predators at the top of a food chain, their prey species are often affected. In Africa, antelope species increase rapidly when leopards and lions are killed. Their increased numbers then surpass the carrying capacity of the habitat, resulting in overgrazed and trampled vegetation followed by starvation.

"What man has done, of course, is remove the natural enemies of the animals he wants to hunt—his beloved target species," wrote Roger Caras (*A Celebration of Cats*, 1986). "He becomes the only real hazard allowed in the system. Without natural enemies, animals do overpopulate, do starve, and do die in unnatural numbers, all because they have been allowed or forced to live in unnatural numbers. No system is in charge because man has destroyed the system."

Trophy hunting has an even more insidious effect on wild populations. It is often the alpha male, the dominant breeder, the animal with the best genes, that is taken for a wall mount. This is especially true of animals that are poached. The removal of such animals, coupled with habitat

loss, only hastens the degradation of wild gene pools, typically among species that are already highly endangered.

POACHING

Fashion Demands Spots

"Oh, but the cat is most admirable," wrote D. J. Bruckner in *Van der Steen's Cats* (1984). "We pay the great ones dreadful tribute, killing them so we can wear their skins, not as Hercules wore the lion's as a sign of strength, but in the ridiculous belief that in a great cat's skin we can look half as good as the cat."

Wearing the fur of dead animals has long been a status symbol. Most recently, photographs of South Africa's Zulu King Goodwill Zwelithini and Inkatha party leader Mangosuthu Buthelezi showed both men wearing leopard-skin capes and headpieces as they addressed their supporters.

Cat skins conjure up images of wealth, stealth, physical prowess, and power—sex appeal. In the 1960s and 1970s fur coats made from spotted cat fur became the rage—and the reason jaguars, cheetahs, and leopards were slaughtered en masse. The spotted and striped cat designs were mimicked in synthetics and used not only to decorate inhabitable interiors but human exteriors. A woman wrapped in cat skin—real or fake—becomes a slinky seductress.

In spite of national and international laws now banning the trade in endangered cat skins, the slaughter of wild felines continues. Fur coats made of spotted cat skins and pelts of snow leopards, jaguars, leopard cats, and clouded leopards still find their way onto the black market. When more than fifty thousand Portuguese soldiers were stationed in Angola and Mozambique, the sale of one leopard skin in Lisbon could more than double their severance pay.

"Far from exploiting a splendid if sustainable source of income, the local people are being induced to cut their throats," wrote Norman Myers (*The World's Cats*, 1976). "As skins become more difficult to obtain, their value increases, providing a bigger incentive to local poachers to hunt down every last spotted cat."

An undercover investigation of Vietnamese wildlife markets funded by the International Primate Protection League (IPPL) in Sommer-

Opposite: **Because cats are associated with intelligence, strength, and power, the right to wear their skins has traditionally been reserved for warriors, royalty, and the wealthy. For example, a Kikuyu witch doctor in Kenya conveys his exalted status by wearing a cheetah skin.**

ville, South Carolina, revealed that Vietnam's precious wildlife is being sold wholesale—dead or alive, at home and abroad—as part of the new liberalized "open door" economic policy. Markets in Ho Chi Minh City offer everything from stuffed tigers, clouded leopards, and leopard cats to cat skins, tiger purses, and other feline body-part souvenirs. Live animals can be purchased as well—for consumption or for export. According to an IPPL newsletter (August 1992), "The Saigon Market is one of the most active places for trading animals and birds in Southeast Asia, if not the world."

And so it is for all developing countries where

THE BUSINESS OF ANIMAL PARTS

Each year trade in wildlife generates an estimated $5 to $8 billion dollars—$2 to $3 billion of it illegal. The United States is the largest consumer of animal exotica—accounting for at least a fifth of all sales.

According to writer Will Baker, the "age of oil" has turned wildlife species into "a limited, rare, and extremely valuable resource . . . a spiritual resource . . . a yearning for the icons of macho primitivism, for the cachet of lust and power that clings to the pelts, claws, horns, or teeth of wild things."

A tour through the six-thousand-square-foot evidence warehouse of the U.S. Fish and Wildlife Service's National Forensics Laboratory in Ashland, Oregon, confirms this. The place is the personification of "creepy." More than three hundred thousand bits and pieces of dead animals bulge from boxes and shelves—a macabre shrine to nature transformed into the bizarre. As if in a Costco's warehouse of animal products, endless blue metal shelves are stacked with stuffed turtles, wild cats, crocodile handbags with head and feet still attached—even rattlesnake tennis shoes. One wall is covered floor-to-ceiling with endless rows of cowboy boots made from every exotic illegal skin imaginable.

A row of stuffed and lacquered sea turtles peers out from a shadowy shelf—one has been fashioned into a guitar. Whole frogs have been converted into coin purses that zip up the tummy. Cat skulls, crocodile-head ashtrays, and rattlesnake penholders sit next to rolls and rolls of python skins. A Grevy's zebra skin collects dust on another shelf, and a roll of gray, rubbery material turns out to be a complete elephant skin. With a sweep of the eye, one can see the world's most threatened and endangered wildlife species—and why they are so.

For four thousand years, animal parts have been an integral part of Chinese medicine. Tied up in mysticism and magic, traditional Asian remedies aim to impart the best qualities—the very spirit of the animal—to the human patient. Under these conditions, admiration can spell doom for coveted creatures such as the tiger. Because of its venerated strength and intelligence, the tiger represents the most powerful animal for cure and prevention in Asia—and

Opposite: Venerated for strength and intelligence, the tiger is considered a pharmaceutical cure-all for those who believe in traditional Asian medicine. As such, tigers are being converted into tiger bone wine, tonic of tiger tail, whisker charms, and tiger-claw jewelry.

people face starvation. Native wildlife represents a resource that can be converted into cash—into food. Unfortunately, it is not the poor local people who benefit from this trade in wildlife. It is the shrewd middlemen, corrupt park or government officials, the retailing foreign businessmen, who often see the biggest profits.

as such, it has been turned into a four-footed pharmacy.

For example, tiger whiskers kept as charms are supposed to ward off bullets and give one courage. Tiger-claw jewelry will protect one from sudden fright. Convulsions in children can be prevented by tying tiger foot bones to their wrists—and in an adult by swallowing a tiger's eyeball. Have a skin disease? Just grind up some tiger tail, mix it with soap, and apply. Having trouble with centipedes? Just burn some tiger hair, and their zillion legs will beat a hasty retreat. And if ghosts have given you a fever, just sit on a tiger skin. While so reclined, why not sip some tiger-bone wine? It's considered a cure-all for everything.

Tigers and rhinoceroses are also being pushed toward extinction due to what Ken Goddard, director of the USFWS forensics lab dubs "the guy problem." One entire wall of the warehouse is devoted to the Asian potions, pills, tonics, and elixirs created to nurture the whims and paranoia of ebbing male virility. Belief in the aphrodisiac powers of tiger penis, tiger bones, and rhino-horn pills called "T-balls" can levy enormous poaching pressure on wild animal populations. Just two decades ago, roughly sixty-thousand black rhinos inhabited Africa. Today, only about twenty-three hundred survive in the wild.

Such wildlife carnage upsets natural balances. Unchecked, it leads to the collapse of entire ecosystems. Environmental author Paul Ehrlich likened the process to rivets popping from an airplane until it finally crashes. People can survive with far fewer wild species, he warned, but eventually even *Homo sapiens* will be at risk.

Recently a renewed interest in animal intelligence has thrown an extra spin on such slaughter, as pointed out by *Time* senior editor Eugene Linden (March 22, 1993). "In 1637 René Descartes described animals as little more than automatons 'sleepwalking through life without a mote of self-awareness.' Two centuries later, Charles Darwin rattled this bastion of *Homo*-centric thinking by arguing that people shared common ancestry with the animal kingdom—that we were related to the very critters that we mocked and exploited.

"If the notion that animals might actually *think* poses a problem," concluded Linden, "it is an ethical one. The great philosophers, such as Descartes, used their belief that animals cannot think as a justification for arguing that they do not have moral rights. It is one thing to treat animals as mere resources if they are presumed to be little more than living robots, but it is entirely different if they are recognized as

A carefully mounted leopard skin is for sale in a South African tourist shop. Even though trade in spotted furs from endangered cat species is now illegal, the killing and the purchases continue.

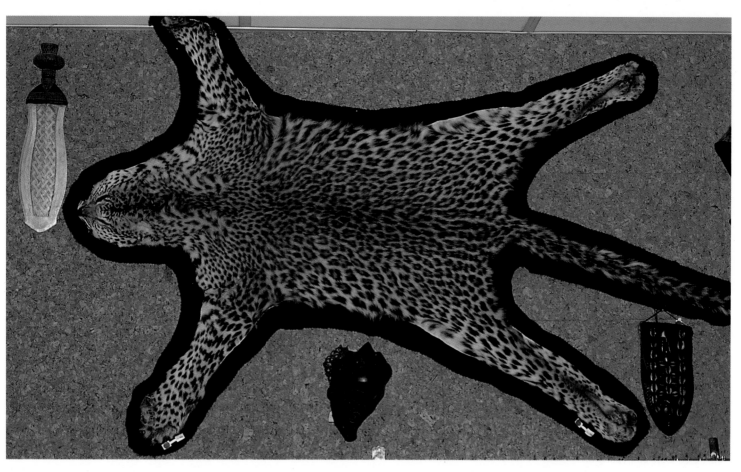

fellow sentient beings. Working out the moral implications," said Linden, "makes a perfect puzzle for a large-brained, highly social species like our own."

TO OWN AN EXOTIC

As if wild cats did not already have it tough enough, many end up on the auction block, as part of the $100-million-a-year "alternative live-stock industry." According to an investigative report in *Audubon* (July 1993) by author Jim Mason, thousands of exotic animals, including endangered species and hybridized oddities, are being auctioned each year from Ohio to Texas.

"Powerful rulers, taking time out from war, collected exotic animals—for their own amuse-ment, to impress foreign visitors, and to display some of the marvels of nature's work," wrote Cliff Tarpy in the July 1993 issue of *National Geographic*. "The number of animals in a royal or private collection, the variety of species, in time came to confer prestige."

Some argue that private ownership of rare and unusual animals has occurred for generations. Others claim an upsurge in the exotics market occurred twenty years ago when zoos started selling excess animals to roadside menageries, breeders, trainers, and private collectors—even private hunting ranches.

According to Mason, lions, cheetahs, leop-ards, small spotted cats on leashes, white tigers, snow leopards, even a hand-raised clouded leop-ard—the most endangered cats can be purchased as part of this booming trade in exotics. North Chinese leopards go for $1,250 to $1,500; snow leopards for $5,000 to $7,000. For $700 you can buy a liger—a cross between a male lion and a female tiger. Or, as one Indiana couple adver-tised, how about cougar cubs as "stocking stuffers" next Christmas?

As the laws are now written, the federal gov-ernment has no jurisdiction over inter- or intrastate trade in exotic endangered animals, meaning those not native to the United States. To buy such a captive-bred exotic, all one needs to do is register with the U.S. Fish and Wildlife

A pair of cheetahs in the Masai Mara Game Reserve of Kenya have been so habituated to tourists that they stand unperturbed on the hood of a Land Rover.

Service. And because hybrids of endangered species are considered nonentities—not recognized or protected by law—the business of privately breeding genetic novelties can go completely unchecked.

What hasn't gone unnoticed is the mounting problems caused by this alternative industry. Escaped pet wolves and cougars have attacked children in Ohio. In Missouri a whole troop of

Japanese macaques infected with a simian herpes virus lethal to humans escaped and roamed free in the Ozark forests before eventual capture.

Escaped exotics can pose a health risk not only to humans, but to native wildlife as well. It is suspected that trade and shipment of raccoons helped spread the current rabies epidemic along the East Coast. When red deer or European elk raised on North American elk ranches for the

Arizona. White-tailed deer may soon have the competitive sika deer from Asia breathing down their backs. Similarly, feral mouflon (sheep), originally from Iran, have held up reintroduction of native bighorn sheep in Oregon because it was feared they had the competitive edge. In Colorado, escaped mouflon have simply interbred with bighorn sheep.

With all of the painstaking effort now being made to monitor the gene pools of both captive and wild endangered species, it is no wonder that zoo and field biologists are up at arms over the runaway breeding and interbreeding of exotics in and out of private collections. While many people who own exotics truly mean well and believe they are helping to save endangered species, what they do not realize is that unless their breeding efforts are recognized and monitored by a program organized by the American Zoo and Aquarium Association (AZA), their animals will be considered genetic dead ends, too genetically contaminated for use in legitimate conservation efforts.

This is just another dimension of the overloaded Ark—caused in part by a people-overloaded planet. As zoos become the last refuge for wildlife caught in a habitat squeeze, even they have limited capacity. According to William Conway, who oversees five New York zoos as part of the Wildlife Conservation Society, all the world's available zoo spaces combined could easily fit within New York City's borough of Brooklyn—and most zoos are already full up. Most facilities rely on animal contraceptives and sterilizations to limit unwanted births. This is likened to playing God—tough decisions are being made that affect not only which species will be saved, which individuals can mate, and when—but which individuals will be euthanized when there is no longer any room on the Ark.

Most controversial has been the selling of exotics to private game ranches that later offer up the animals to paying customers in "canned hunts"—the killing of tame and semitame animals in a confined space. According to writer Ted Williams (*Audubon*, January/February 1992), in Texas alone there are nearly five hundred game ranches, where you can kill the exotic trophy of your choice, in the enclosure of your choice. There, if you have $3,000 to $5,000 to burn, it's possible to organize a cat shoot in just forty minutes. Of the roughly 14 million hunters in America, approximately 500,000 patronize

Asian horn market escape, they not only hybridize with the native species, but also run the risk of spreading bovine tuberculosis.

Most alarming, when these Noah's Ark aliens escape—or are released—they hit the ground running, often outcompeting native species for food and turf. Barbary sheep, a potential threat to bighorn sheep, now run free in the southwestern United States and can be shot on sight in

Two sand cat kittens (*Felis margarita*) cuddle together. Endangered in the wild and difficult to breed in captivity, species of small wild cats such as these are hard to protect. Very little is known about the behavioral ecology of most small felid species in the wild. Few are adequately represented in captive breeding collections.

game ranches and preserves for what has been dubbed "stop and pop" shopping for game—hunts of often tame, trusting, declawed exotic pets and surplused zoo animals.

The Humane Society of the United States has castigated such hunts as "a form of sport hunting stripped of all conservation values—a commercial enterprise whose merchandise is the 'pleasure' of killing" (*Animals,* January/February 1992). Not only are thousands of animals killed in this manner on North American game ranches each year, but such ranches complicate efforts to control poaching. Illegally obtained meat and wildlife parts can easily be laundered through them.

According to Mason, the trade in exotics raises ethical issues about our wheeling and dealing with live animals. "Should wild species be selectively bred to make docile, cute pets?" he asks. "Should we propagate miniature animals and other mutations for our amusement? Should endangered species be farmed so that everyone can own a last piece of the wild?"

It would seem that people's fascination with the rare and the genetically bizarre—the zedonks, ligers, zorses, and fainting goats—is fueled by the same drives that produce tiger-skin purses, elephant-foot umbrella holders, and rattlesnake tennis shoes. Animals pay dearly for such whimsy—with loss of dignity, but most often with their lives.

CATS AS VERMIN

Food Chain Politics

Curious impartial sympathy toward all creatures, regardless of their diet, is an attitude of the cultivated mind.

—*DURWARD ALLEN,*

Our Wildlife Legacy, 1954

If not economically exploited for their body parts, wild cats have been exterminated outright as "vermin." They have been poisoned, trapped, shot, and clubbed to death as predatory rivals for game species—and as alleged drains on livestock profits. In South and Central America, any jaguar *suspected* of killing livestock was eliminated—no

proof required. In the United States, jaguarundi were trapped and poisoned as poultry thieves, and bounties were placed on the heads of North American cougars. Up until the 1930s, the government even poisoned and shot cougars and wolves right inside our national parks.

The rampant sentiments of predator hatred *en vogue* at the turn of the century were eloquently expressed by President Theodore Roosevelt when he described a treed cougar as "the big horse-killing cat, the destroyer of the deer, the lord of stealthy murder, facing his doom with a heart both craven and cruel."

In Southwest Africa, some impassioned farmers went so far as to take poisoned chunks of meat into the Namib Kalahari Gemsbok National Park in hopes of killing park predators before they escaped park boundaries to kill livestock. The African lion was once considered vermin and shot indiscriminately by farmers, hunters, and game personnel throughout their range. As a result of such pressure, the Gir Sanctuary in India protects the last remnant population of Asiatic lions. With most of their prey base destroyed, their main source of food is now cattle.

"Hunting predators is a tough and challenging sport," wrote hunter Andy Cline in *Outdoor Life.* "It blends the calling skill of turkey hunting with the thrill-of-the-chase excitement of big-game hunting. Although coyotes are the most numerous and easily hunted of the predators, hunters can also take bobcats, gray foxes and red foxes in many areas. Each is called to the gun by imitating wounded prey on a call."

According to Cline, the challenge is to imitate the call of a small, wounded animal, making it sound "as pathetic and sad as possible." One can use a rabbit squealer to produce the plaintive calls, or purchase any number of tapes that teach how to make the calls yourself with hands cupped to mouth. "Fencerows, treelines, haystacks and brush piles make good cover," advised Cline.

Historically, efforts to protect the cougar throughout the western states have been met with opposition from the cattle industry—and hunters. In Arizona people still shoot cougars on sight, and in Texas there is an open season on them. At issue even more than livestock economics is a deep-rooted frontier psyche—a wild and free conquesting way of life where men were men and the only good predator was a dead one. Bears, wolves, coyotes, cougars, bobcats, birds of prey—any animal that competed with people was

A puma (*Felis concolor*) in Belize shows the species' versatility of habitat. These large cats can be found from sea level to fifteen thousand feet, from brush country to tropical forest.

eliminated. Even today, an estimated eighteen hundred cougars are still killed each year in the western United States as pests and trophies.

"Deliberate war on any species . . . diminishes, endangers, and brutalizes us," wrote Wallace Stegner in the forward to the book *Cougar: Ghost of the Rockies* (1993). "If we cannot live in harmony with other forms of life, if we cannot control our hostility toward the earth and its creatures, how shall we ever learn to control our hostility toward each other?"

In 1990, when Proposition 117 passed in California banning mountain lion trophy hunts, hunters were up at arms. "Rural folks couldn't understand why anyone would want to legislate a ban on mountain lion hunting," wrote Jim Matthews (*Outdoor Life*, March 1991). "It was a right, like owning guns. You hunted lions to keep their population down so they didn't eat your pet dog or yearling colt or too many of the deer you hunted in the fall; you hunted them because it was in your blood and was something you did."

The important role predators play in managing prey populations was illustrated naturally in Arizona earlier this century. Beginning in 1906, when predators were eliminated from Arizona's Kaibab Plateau, the white-tailed deer population expanded from four thousand to a hundred thousand in less than twenty years. Left unchecked, the deer eventually outgrew the carrying capacity of their habitat, and with vegetation stripped, thousands died from starvation. After the population crash, only about ten thousand deer remained.

"It is a natural function of predators to keep big-game range from being destroyed by the animals it supports," wrote biologist Durward Allen in his book *Our Wildlife Legacy* (1954).

Field research conducted by Maurice Hornocker and others has shown that cougars are not detrimental to game species (*Los Angeles Times Magazine,* March 1, 1992). In fact, they serve an important role in culling out the old, weak, and sick animals, and preventing the spread of disease. Smaller feline species help keep rodents and insects in check. The few large cats that do attack livestock are often old or injured cats—or those whose primary prey base has been destroyed.

"All wild animals are indicator species," warned retired U.S. Fish and Wildlife employee Frank Kenney, "and, when one or another starts to drop out of the race, something is very wrong with our environment. We, too, are in this race for survival."

NATURAL DISASTERS

Across vast areas of southern Africa, the drought of 1992 caused trees to turn white and riverbeds to dry up and crack into artistic patterns of thirst. Everywhere, grasses burned away, leaving stark moonscapes of bare earth. Tens of thousands of emaciated giraffes and zebras, wildebeests and antelope rested in the hot shade to conserve energy. Hippos dried up and died along with their mud holes. The stench of rotting animal carcasses filled the air.

As the drought progressed, people battled to save the wildlife. From South Africa to Zimbabwe, game rangers used helicopters and trucks to rescue hundreds of hippos, elephants, buffalo, and rhinoceroses from starvation—moving them to greener pastures and running rivers. Farmers shelterd thousands more.

Buffalo were fed intravenously on one South African game reserve. On another, crocodiles stranded in dry riverbeds were airlifted to new homes. In Zimbabwe trucks filled with soybeans, grass, and hay from the north arrived daily to keep thousands of animals alive. Wildlife experts were forced to shoot two thousand elephants and herd one thousand others to new sources of food. More than fifteen hundred buffalo were selectively shot in the Gonarezhou National Park to try to save the hundreds that remained.

The catastrophic drought began in January 1992, when the rains suddenly stopped. Far worse than the drought of 1983, when thousands of cattle and wild animals died, this drought was called the drought of the century, the worst since 1896. Lack of water, barren prairies, and man-made fences combined to endanger the lives of wild animals that had once been abundant. The hardest hit area was near Zimbabwe's border with South Africa and Mozambique—one of the richest remaining refuges for wildlife.

The drought illustrated how vulnerable wildlife can be, even when protected in parks and preserves that are, in effect, giant zoos encircled by fences. These wildlife "islands" can suddenly become too small during droughts that can last a year or more. Historically wildlife survived during such lean times by migrating to better areas for food and water. With escape blocked, and overflow areas converted to agriculture, wildlife reserves can quickly become wildlife death traps without human intervention.

Wild fires can also wipe out parks and protected species. In 1994, AZA director of science Michael Hutchins visited Brazil's 326,000-acre Emas National Park shortly after 99 percent of it was destroyed by an uncontrollable fire. "It looked like a desolate moonscape," said Hutchins. "The loss of wildlife was extraordinary—maned wolves, bush dogs, giant anteaters, and blue and gold macaws. The wildlife that remained seemed in shock. The lack of cover provided a rare opportunity to see a puma walking through the charred landscape."

In 1994, dozens of lions suddenly died in Tanzania's Serengeti National Park. The mysterious epidemic, which caused convulsions in the big cats, was diagnosed as canine distemper. Entire prides were wiped out—once again under-scoring the vulnerability of animals to disease, even when protected.

As documented by Mark and Delia Owens during their seven-year study of Botswana's Kalahari lions (*International Wildlife*, September/October 1984), during severe drought, desert lions abandon their territories, separate from their pridemates, and roam areas as much as fifteen times larger than their wet-season ranges. They survive for months without water by killing smaller prey and drinking the blood and body fluids from each carcass.

The drought that occurred in the Pacific Northwest during 1992 wasn't as severe, but still caused the movement of deer and other animals, including cougars, closer to places inhabited by people. Near Enumclaw, Washington, a cougar attacked a child who was camping with his father. The boy wasn't seriously hurt. In Washington, another attack occurred near Lake Wenatchee, on a young girl. According to Jim Rieck (*Everett Herald Highlights*, July 1, 1992), program manager and wildlife biologist for the state Department of Wildlife, children tend to attract cougars because of their size and activity—just as a mouse attracts a cat.

Cougars normally avoid people by being most active in the early morning hours and at dusk. There have been only four documented cases in the State of Washington of people being attacked by cougars—two of them in 1992. According to Rieck, drought brings humans and cougars into contact. When deer, elk, and other game migrate to creeks and lakes in search of water, the predatory cougars also follow. People like to congregate around creeks and lakes when it is hot and dry, and so do thirsty wild animals.

What should you do if you encounter a cougar? "Stay calm," advises Rieck. "The worst thing you can do is turn and run, an act that provokes predatory behavior. Make yourself look larger than you are. Stand on your toes, hold a walking stick or fishing pole over your head while slowly backing away, and keep an eye on the cat. If you're with a child, take the child in your arms, or even put the child on your shoulders, instructing the child to remain still. And if all else fails and a cougar becomes aggressive," says Rieck, "throw sticks and rocks at it while continuing to back away."

In spite of such reports, most of us will never encounter a cougar in the wild—much less any wild cats, other than possibly a feral house cat.

In recent years, loss of habitat and drought have brought cougars in more frequent contact with people. It is best to learn how to travel safely in cougar country *before* you go. Young children are most at risk.

6

Wild Cat Conservation

WHAT IS BEING DONE

Animals are among the conductors of life's greatest symphonies. They exist not solely

for our convenience or fancy, but are an important rhythm to the planet we share.

—*DARCY BELL SYMES, Animals Magazine, 1981*

iologist Randy Eaton was one of the first to publicize the need for increased research and conservation of wild cats. According to Eaton, when wild felines are protected, their entire biota is preserved. Conservation of top-level carnivores should, therefore, be a primary goal in order to preserve the sensitive food-chain dynamics of fragile ecosystems. But such efforts can only succeed with adequate knowledge of a species' habitat and prey requirements, social organization, and mortality and recruitment rates, and such knowledge does not come easily. It can only be obtained through long-term field research on each individual species.

That's the hitch in feline conservation. George Schaller in the 1970s popularized his early study of African lions, a highly visible species. Maurice Hornocker published his first paper on mountain lion ecology in 1968. His difficult study of an elusive large cat was made easier with the use of radio telemetry, then a relatively new technology which made it possible to follow the movement of wild animals with radio signals. Just twenty years ago, as the big African and Asian cats were being studied, nothing more than short-term studies had been conducted on any South American cats.

While many of the big cats have now been studied, and millions of dollars are being invested in their conservation and captive breeding, the majority of the smaller species have not fared as well. Of the thirty-seven species of wild felines, most are small and nocturnal, and many are arboreal, making them more difficult to study in the wild. It is much harder to raise research funds for invisible species about which little is known than to raise money to study, say, the lion or cheetah. It has also proven more difficult to breed these secretive smaller species in captivity.

A SUMMIT FOR CATS

In 1991, in an effort to publicize the environmental crisis affecting the world's diverse species of cats, the American Zoo and Aquarium Association (AZA) and the World

Above: Cheetahs are as genetically identical as inbred lab mice, which makes these endangered cats highly vulnerable to disease and reproductive problems.

Opposite: A bobcat (*Lynx rufus*) hides among ferns in the Hoh River rain forest of Washington's Olympic National Park. Ranging from southern Canada to central Mexico, the bobcat is still widely found throughout much of the United States.

Conservation Union (WCU) cosponsored an inaugural Felid Action Planning Meeting at Front Royal, Virginia, to share facts about the current status of both wild and captive felines—and to establish ambitious objectives for their global conservation. Following this meeting, the availability of all space for captive felids was assessed via survey of institutions accredited with the AZA. Specific felid species were chosen for intensive management from Africa, Asia, and North and South America. In North America, these species included the Florida panther, Texas ocelot, bobcats, and the North American lynx and puma. Finally, a list of top-priority research projects was selected for immediate funding.

Of the 37 species recognized by the WCU and AZA (*Felid Action Plan*, 1991/1992) within the family *Felidae*, 91 percent of all species and subspecies were recommended for research; 76 percent were considered threatened with extinction; 12 percent were listed as critical; 29 percent as endangered; and 34 percent as vulnerable. At the time of publication, only 24 percent were considered safe.

WILDLIFE SANCTUARIES

A study conducted by Wyoming Fish and Game calculated that wildlife preserved for viewing is worth three times more than wildlife managed for hunting. Because we will spend a great deal of money to see animals in the wild, and many more people are moving to areas where they can be closer to nature, the presence of wildlife can encourage economic development.

The feasibility of using tourism to promote the conservation of wild cats is more complicated, because the majority of the *Felidae* are difficult to see in the wild. Much of their remaining wild habitat is located in areas that are inaccessible, or in areas that are coveted by farmers, herdsmen, or loggers. However, if we protect habitat for wild cats, we will also protect other, more visible species of birds and mammals that may have greater tourist appeal.

The essence of felid conservation is best summarized by Richard Poelker, who studied the status of cougars in Washington State. "It is important to realize that the value of a puma to some is simply the knowledge that it exists, that it is 'out there' somewhere making its way," says Poelker, "even if that person is just sitting at

home in front of a fire, or watching a puma special on television. Not only is it important to consider these indirect or vicarious nonconsumptive uses, but to incorporate them into management plans. Every game and non-game animal has its own intrinsic and esthetic value."

BELIZE—A MODEL FOR CAT CONSERVATION

In 1981 Belize declared a moratorium on all hunting of jaguars. Three years later, the progressive government designated one hundred thousand acres of the Cockscomb Basin as the world's first jaguar reserve. A no-hunting ban was extended to all wildlife within the area, protecting the jaguar and four other species of wild cats as well as their prey. In 1989 the entire basin gained sanctuary status and was renamed the Cockscomb Basin Wildlife Sanctuary.

Surrounded on three sides by rugged mountains, the Cockscomb Basin has avoided most of the ravages of expanding human populations due to its geographic isolation. Within the sanctuary, there are hundreds of streams, three river systems, the 3,300-foot Victoria Peak, and a rich flora and fauna, including 55 species of mammals and 290 species of birds. Brocket deer, anteaters, two species of peccaries, and the endangered, horse-sized Biard's tapir inhabit the forest, along with ocelots, margays, jaguarundis, pumas, and jaguars. Recently a group of black howler monkeys was reintroduced into the sanctuary, the original population having been wiped out by hunting, hurricanes, and yellow fever.

The Cockscomb Basin Wildlife Sanctuary is one of the few places on earth inhabited by five different species of cats. Initial studies by felid specialist Alan Rabinowitz, of the Wildlife Conservation Society in New York, revealed how each species utilizes a different part of the same habitat. The forty-pound ocelot catches ground-dwelling prey such as armadillos, opossums, peccaries, and small deer. The nocturnal, arboreal margay finds its food in the trees, feeding on birds and rodents. Weasel-like jaguarundis hunt along forest edges, ranging widely to dine on rodents, amphibians, birds—even fruit. And the two-hundred-pound jaguars can easily kill the six-hundred-pound tapirs, but usually prey on smaller mammals, such as deer, peccaries, and armadillos. To date, the elusive puma, or "red

A female leopard (*Panthera pardus*) carries a freshly killed impala kid through the dense woodlands along the Samburu River. Leopards will often climb trees, pulling their prey away from other predators, which often gang up on a single leopard.

tiger," has been sighted in the Cockscomb but evaded study.

The Cockscomb Wildlife Sanctuary has proven a viable model for cat conservation. Since the area was protected, not only have there been increased sightings of jaguars within the reserve, but fewer jaguar problems reported outside of it. By protecting the jaguar, the sanctuary has provided umbrella protection for all other endemic species within it. Every effort is now being made to economically integrate the local Maya Indians into the development of ecotourism in the area, as well as sanctuary management. Several Maya men are employed as sanctuary wardens and watchmen, and former Maya schoolteacher Ernesto Saqui is the sanctuary director, acting as liaison between the local Maya people and the numerous international conservation groups and Belizean authorities that helped establish the sanctuary.

To date, the Belizean government has committed 30 percent of its landmass to no-hunting sanctuaries, creating more than six hundred thousand acres of private and public reserves and sanctuaries. As a result of effective public education campaigns, many citrus farmers have stopped posting bounties on jaguars and have begun preserving sections of private forest as corridors for jaguars and other wildlife.

TANZANIA—MAKING WILDLIFE SELF-SUPPORTING

Selous Game Park protects some of the last truly wild areas left in Africa. Its impenetrable forests, ten-foot-high grass, mountains, and gorges are as close to virgin Africa as one can experience. Encompassing twenty thousand square miles, it is one of the world's biggest reserves—bigger than the country of Switzerland.

Once a hundred thousand elephants roamed the park. Today only about thirty thousand remain, due to poaching. Wildlife protection costs money, but because of the park's enormous size, it is not suited for photo safaris. The income generated from the two thousand tourists who visit the park each year is negligible.

To help raise the much-needed conservation funds required to run the park, the German Society for Technical Cooperation (GSTC) in Selous oversees limited big-game hunts. Each year about 120 big-game hunters each pay an average of $30,000 for a Selous hunting safari. It costs $4,000 to shoot an elephant and $2,000 to kill a lion or leopard—excluding the whopping hunting licenses and safari fees. "Anyone who books a big-game safari is paying for an illusion," claims Rolf Baldus, head of GSTC. "Many of those that book an elephant hunt don't shoot a single tusker," because no elephants can be found, or they are just too small to shoot.

Until 1989, poachers slaughtered five thousand elephants a year. Only ten elephants were legally killed in the park in 1991, compared to a thousand elephants killed during the same period by local farmers protecting their crops.

Big-game hunting is the most important source of income in Selous. In 1990 hunting fees generated more than $1 million to help run the park and combat poaching.

IN-COUNTRY TRAINING

After years of physical and financial support from other countries, wildlife officials from developing countries now realize that the only way they can help guarantee long-term protection for their wildlife resources is to learn how to do it themselves. The result is that local personnel need management and conservation training from foreign countries, not conservation rhetoric. They need the commitment of time and energy to learn these skills.

To that end, the MacArthur Foundation funded Alan Rabinowitz and Elizabeth Bennett through the Wildlife Conservation Society to develop training curricula for both junior and senior wildlife staff, to be field-tested for two years in the East Malaysian states of Sabah and Sarawak. Short, intensive courses were also taught in southern China and Taiwan.

According to Rabinowitz, senior staff received training in long-term planning, problem solving, leadership skills, and efficient utilization of junior personnel. Junior staff received technical training on the use of data sheets, animal identification, compasses, survey techniques, interviewing skills, and track and sign identification. The training

included homework, group discussions, videos, participation in field surveys—and final exams.

As a first step toward helping governments take responsibility for their own wildlife, the training program was successful. At the same time, it also helped establish data collection and monitoring programs for key wildlife areas within each country. To ensure that the results are long-lasting, comprehensive training syllabuses have been translated into the national language of each country so that the recently graduated senior and junior wildlife personnel can continue the ongoing process of training in-country staff.

ZOOS AS PRESERVES

When wildlife was plentiful, zoos were literally menageries: odd collections of the planet's most unusual creatures displayed behind bars and glass, meant to entertain more than to educate. In the past twenty years, as the rate of habitat loss and wildlife extinctions has accelerated, the role of zoos has shifted to reflect these trends. Gone are the amusement rides and circus atmosphere. Zoos still make it possible to see the world's most exotic wonders—from Siberian tigers and California condors to giant pandas and the rare snow leopard—but now the animals are displayed with greater dignity. Visitors can experience a rain forest, watch polar bears swim underwater, or gaze across an African savanna to get a taste of wilderness as well as wildlife.

Now instead of competing for the greatest number of species, zoos are displaying fewer species but in larger, more naturalistic habitats. Better educational graphics reflect the current conservation ethic and explain the significance of both the animal and its habitat and how they are both faring in the wild. There is a greater urgency now about not only seeing these animals, but also protecting and breeding them in captivity. For many endangered species, zoos have become the last stop on a quick trip to extinction; a sole survivor may linger for years and, at best, may only leave frozen eggs, semen, or DNA behind before disappearing altogether.

SPECIES DATABASES

In 1979, National Zoo research scientist Katherine Ralls used a computer model to predict that if no changes were made in captive management, zoo animals would become so inbred and unhealthy that they could possibly die out within 150 years. Heeding Ralls's warning, the AZA created the Species Survival Plan (SSP). Each SSP formulates a "master plan" outlining which animals within a captive population should breed, when, how often, and with whom. Studbook keepers play a critical role in this plan. They maintain detailed, up-to-date databases on specific animal populations, including each individual's age, sex, and reproductive history. Currently over 230 studbooks are maintained under the auspices of AZA.

The International Species Information System (ISIS), located in Apple Valley, Minnesota, maintains a registry of animals held by participating zoos and aquariums around the world. ISIS supplies two computer packages to zoo and aquarium managers: ARKS (Animal Records Keeping System), which allows insitutions to record and submit their animal inventory to the central database, and SPARKS (Single Population Analysis and Record Keeping System), which assists managers with the analyses needed to use studbook records to formulate SSP master plans. Such plans maximize retention of genetic diversity by identifying the best pairings possible. To date, 70 SSP programs have been initiated for 117 of the world's most endangered species, each with its own coordinator and management group. Thanks to the institutional registrars, the records of more than *one million* animals have also been processed into the ISIS database. ISIS now contains basic census information on captive animals held at 400 institutions located on every continent except Antarctica. Approximately 5,500 living felid specimens are registered with ISIS.

Prompted by horse thievery, Wyoming rancher Vern Taylor worked with microchip engineers to develop an injectable microchip, or transponder, about the size of a pencil point. An encoded copper coil inside each chip generates a unique ten-digit readout when a wand is passed over it—much like the I.D. bar codes used in a supermarket. Unlike tattooing and branding, which can be altered, the microchip application is quick and accurate, and identification is exact and permanent. Labs and zoos are now using transponders to keep track of individual animals.

Collectively, these databases and high-tech I.D. tags make it possible to trace wild felids held by professionally managed zoological parks. Such information is invaluable in monitoring the dwindling gene pools of endangered cat species and in planning captive breeding programs to maximize their genetic diversity. The information is also important in planning the best use of an estimated eleven thousand "spaces" available for captive felids in all world zoos.

WILDLIFE CORRIDORS

When field biologists first started studying animals in the wild, the technology available was primitive. Armed with binoculars, notepad, pencil, and some good hiking shoes, scientists did their best to catch glimpses of their wild subjects. Field conditions were often tough, and the resulting wildlife portraits were limited.

Then came the use of radio waves and satellite "eyes" to spy on animals. With the use of radio telemetry and high-tech satellite sleuthing, our knowledge about the behavior, ecology, and movements of animals has increased dramatically. One of the biggest surprises was to learn just how far-ranging many animals are, as well as the location of their most critical habitats. Knowledge about migration routes and refueling stops, and areas used for feeding, wintering over, and reproduction have helped to change earlier views on wildlife conservation. We now know that most large predators need enormous tracts of land in order to find adequate food and mates, and to successfully reproduce, and that these island habitats need to be interconnected in order to maintain a healthy gene flow between populations. Where they exist, wildlife corridors between parks have helped relieve population pressure on both animals and overused habitat. Where they don't exist, the ensuing problems with overcrowding, habitat destruction, and gene flow have resulted in expensive intervention.

According to Jared Diamond (*Natural History,* August 1992), "to combat the risk of inbreeding and promote exchange of genes, South Africa's conservation agencies now devote a substantial fraction of their budget to airlifting rhinos and other large mammals between reserves."

When wild animals attempt to disperse without such assistance, they often run head-on into civilization. For example, only thirty to fifty endangered panthers survive in Florida. Speeding automobiles have turned into their most lethal enemies, killing at least one a year. To help

Only since the 1960s, when the first field studies of big cats were begun by George Schaller and Maurice Hornocker, did people begin to take a serious interest in the behavior and conservation of wild cats. The great cats, such as this lion cub in Kenya, have now been well studied. It is the small, little-known felid species that need immediate attention.

reduce the feline fatalities occurring along a 40-mile stretch of Alligator Alley Highway, which cuts right through the Everglades, the Florida Department of Transportation has constructed custom-built tunnels beneath the asphalt. In the meantime, land purchases made by the Nature Conservancy have protected more than thirty thousand acres of panther habitat throughout the Everglades.

INNOVATIVE CAPTIVE BREEDING EFFORTS

Most people are aware of the global efforts being made to protect endangered species. But in a few laboratories across the country, far more subtle, more pervasive forms of "intervention" are now taking place. High-tech biomedical efforts are being made to assess and computerize population gene pools, genetically fingerprint individual species, establish species "studbooks," and collect and freeze sperm and fertilized eggs (embryos) from endangered species.

"Ultimately, sperm banking, artificial insemination, in vitro fertilization, and embryo transfers may be the only hope for many animals doomed to extinction," says Betsy Dresser, director of research at the Cincinnati Zoo's Center for Reproduction of Endangered Species (CREW). "It's now a race against the clock to protect existing gene pools."

A diverse gene pool is the basis on which evolution progresses through the process of natural selection. Yet inbreeding reduces genetic diversity with alarming results. Infertility, birth defects, increased juvenile mortality, and an inability to combat infectious disease are typical end products of liaisons between siblings, mother and son, or father and daughter.

Realizing the far-reaching implications of a diminished gene pool, scientists are now traveling the world to wrangle biological samples from healthy, wild animals. Endocrine tests of urine or stool samples, collected without anesthesia, can reveal hormones that indicate stress, estrus, the animal's breeding cycle, even the date of an anticipated birth. Genetic analysis of blood and tissue samples can shed light on the health, reproductive state, and genetic status of individual animals and populations—as well as of species as a whole.

Utilizing advances made in cryopreservation and artificial insemination, sperm of endangered species is now being frozen and stored to preserve DNA sequences threatened with extinction, and to prevent inbreeding crises in zoo populations. In fact, frozen sperm from free-living endangered species is now being used to boost the genetic diversity of captive species. As demonstrated with livestock, frozen sperm can be held for decades and still produce live offspring. Such technology is meant to enhance, not replace, living populations.

The collection, storage, and use of germ plasm is part of an emerging technology referred to as "gamete rescue." It is now possible to retrieve viable oocytes and sperm from the reproductive organs of livestock and zoo and laboratory animals that are pronounced clinically dead.

"The potential of this frozen germ plasm has already been demonstrated," explains David Wildt (*Felid Action Plan*, 1991/1992). "We have produced living offspring from five wild felid species. Particularly significant is the recent birth of two leopard cat kittens from the use of frozen, thawed sperm."

Hormone therapy is also being used on captive exotics, such as rhinos, to evaluate the possibility of using superovulation and embryo transfer technology. According to the Cincinnati Zoo's Dresser, large numbers of embryos may be recovered from a single donor female through the use of hormone injections which cause the ovaries to superovulate. The fertilized eggs are then collected with a uterine flush and transferred into a host of surrogate mothers. Once implanted in the uterus, each egg is then carried to term.

In 1986 Cincinnati produced the first litter of domestic cats born from frozen embryos. Soon after, a rare Indian desert wild cat was produced following embryo transfer and gestation in a domestic cat. Embryo transfer, where the embryo of one animal is surgically or nonsurgically inserted into the uterus of another—makes it possible for one species to bear the young of another, for a slow-breeding species to produce many offspring in a year, for a small population to increase rapidly.

In 1992 the Cincinnati research team produced the world's first kitten litters from in vitro fertilized domestic cat embryos that were first frozen, thawed, and then transferred to surrogates. In 1994 they produced the first domestic kitten from an egg that had been injected with a single sperm—a technique that promises great hope for exotic, endangered cat species in which the males often have low sperm counts. The team is now working on trying to unlock the secrets of egg maturation, hoping to stimulate eggs to develop in vitro to the fertilization stage. This would make it possible to save far more eggs gathered from exotic animals, including those collected posthumously from valuable zoo animals that suddenly die.

PROTECTION FOR CATS

In 1993 the National Audubon Society, the Humane Society of the United States, and Defenders of Wildlife joined forces with nine other environmental groups to help protect a threatened population of North American lynx. Only about twenty-five lynx are thought to remain in Washington's Okanogan County. According to biologist Deborah Ferber (*Seattle Times*, April 4, 1993), they probably represent the most viable breeding population south of the Canadian border. Accelerated logging in the area has not only reduced their habitat, but that of their main prey, the snowshoe hare, which lives in fifteen- to forty-year-old forests. Proposed logging and road-building in state and federal forests between Washington's Methow and Okanogan rivers now threaten the remaining habitat of the lynx. Logging roads would also provide better access for poachers.

Armed with satellite images of Okanogan County and field data to support their claims, the groups sued the U.S. Fish and Wildlife Service after the agency rejected a petition to list the subpopulation as endangered. According to the environmentalists, the satellite photos show that extensive clear-cut logging in southern British Columbia has now physically isolated the small remaining lynx population in Okanogan County from a larger population in Canada. Expensive, time-consuming efforts to reintroduce lynx to their former range in the Adirondack Mountains of New York—after they were eliminated through deforestation and habitat invasion by bobcats—suggest that it may be more time- and cost-effective to protect the Okanogan lynx while they are still naturally in place.

IMPROVED LAW ENFORCEMENT

In 1989 the U.S. Fish and Wildlife Service opened a $4.5 million Wildlife Forensics Lab in Ashland, Oregon, the first and only full-service animal crime lab and wildlife identification facility in the world. The 23,000-square-foot lab caters not only to the needs of 210 USFWS agents, 85 wildlife inspectors, and 7,500 game wardens and conservation officers working throughout the United States, but it supports the investigative needs of the 122 countries that have signed the Convention on International Trade in Endangered Species (CITES).

Since opening, the Wildlife Forensics Lab has made several investigative breakthroughs that will make it easier to link criminal, wildlife victim, and crime scene for prosecution. Armed with a $250,000 scanning electron microscope designed by Scotland Yard, a research team headed by forensic scientist Ed Espinoza figured out how to differentiate between legal ancient mammoth and mastodon ivory and mislabeled Asian and African elephant ivory sold illegally on the black market, through microscopic differences in dentinal tubules. The team also discovered that many of the gallbladders sold in Asian medicinal markets as coveted bear gallbladders were in fact from domestic pigs. Most recently, Espinoza's group discovered how to "fingerprint" bullets using the electron microscope and fractal mathematics. Now individual bullets can be matched to the weapon that fired them by computer, which scans them for telltale marks.

With electrophoresis, immunology, and DNA-fingerprinting techniques, lab forensic specialist Steven Fain can take tissue from a wildlife product and identify not only the species, but often the gender—occasionally to a specific animal.

"If we get blood under a fingernail," says senior forensic specialist Peter Dratch (*Animals,* September/October, 1993), "it is enough to identify a species. We can now match blood found at a kill site to blood on a jacket or a car."

The lab is even working on eternity. Blood and tissue cultures from every species possible are being preserved at -80°C. (-112°F.) in enormous liquid nitrogen freezers. From such carefully cataloged samples, the lab can then replicate several billion copies of any desired DNA strand.

"Ironically, DNA fingerprinting may hasten the demise of some species," says lab director Ken Goddard. "Under the current U.S. Endangered Species Act, hybrids do not qualify for protection even if the novel plants or animals produced are vulnerable to extinction."

For example, Thomas Whitham of Northern Arizona University in Flagstaff found that plant hybrids harbor more insects and a greater diversity of insect species than their parents. As a result of this and other research on plant hybrids, Whitham now argues that plant hybrid zones can represent focal points of insect biodiversity and, for that reason alone, should be preserved. Similar merits may be found for mammalian hybrids if laws such as the Endangered Species Act can be rewritten in time to protect them.

In 1993, U.S. Secretary of the Interior Bruce Babbitt merged the biological research and survey activities of eight departmental bureaus into a new National Biological Survey (NBS) "to gather, analyze and disseminate the biological information necessary for the long-term stewardship of our nation's natural resources, and to foster understanding of biological systems and the benefits they provide to society."

Goddard would like the NBS not only to count species but also to come up with legal definitions for each one that includes a genetic component. "The salmon, wolf and Florida panther are examples of what's coming," says Goddard. Everything is going to have a legal ramification. If you can't legally define what a species is, you can't protect it. The laws as written may not be enforceable without a defined genetic range for each protected species—and subspecies.

As competition for land and natural resources increases, emphasis will continue to shift from biological to political issues. Whereas the USFWS Wildlife Forensics Lab initially did well collecting feathers, fur, and teeth to help identify and protect wildlife victims, that may no longer be enough, as shrewd realtors, politicians, and defense attorneys look for loopholes in the Endangered Species Act. Conservation battles have suddenly moved into the political realm of genetics.

ENDANGERED SPECIES ACT UNDER FIRE

"The Endangered Species Act of 1973, perhaps more than any other environmental law, dares to draw an unwavering line in the path of American progress," wrote Tom Horton (*Audubon,*

Small species of cats, such as the margay (*Felis wiedii*), are difficult to study in the wild. Not only are they nocturnal, but they inhabit tropical rain forests, where there is limited visibility. Even so, every effort needs to be made to study these and other small felids in the wild before their habitat is further degraded.

March/April 1992). "It boldly says, in essence, 'Thou shalt not cause any species of plant or animal to go extinct.' As the rampant transformation of natural America . . . pushes more and more species to the wall, the act is embroiled in controversy unparalleled since its passage."

According to Horton, determining whether a species is in danger of extinction has little to do with jobs and dollars and everything to do with biology. The intent of the act is to allow wildlife the space needed to continue evolving, in as many different locations as possible, and to prevent elimination by natural disasters. At issue are the ways we live, farm, log, and obtain energy, many of which are ultimately insupportable. In a conflict pitting bucks against biology, short-term gain against long-term survival, the Endangered Species Act tweaks both conscience and common sense, yet as a single, underfunded law, it serves as but a thumb in a leaky dike.

"So far," said Horton, "it is the Endangered Species Act that is forcing society to confront the mess it has created here. It was a law intended only to provide a last-ditch defense for the most vulnerable plants and animals, not to save the planet—but it sounds a warning for more than just gnatcatchers and kangaroo rats."

CORPORATE HELP

In 1985, when Coca-Cola Foods purchased 197,000 acres of land in Belize to convert to citrus groves, environmentalists hit the roof. Their conservation appeal paid off. In 1988 Coca-Cola Foods donated 40,000 acres of land to the Belize and Massachusetts Audubon Societies to establish a new forest preserve. The company also pledged $50,000 to help acquire additional land and to train people to manage the preserve. Coca-Cola Foods also agreed to donate another 10,000 acres to the Belize government for farming, and 1,700 acres for a tapir breeding project managed by the Belize Zoo. Having abandoned its plans for citrus groves, the company decided to sell or donate all but 50,000 of its acres.

The Ralston Purina Company has also pitched in to help wild cats by establishing their Big Cat Survival Fund. In a corporate program called "Little Cats Helping Big Cats," a percentage of all proceeds from the sales of Purina cat food is being donated to the American Zoo and Aquarium Association to help feline field research and captive breeding efforts. By 1994, more than $600,000 had been donated.

INDIVIDUALS CAN MAKE A DIFFERENCE

"For the first time in human history," wrote Maitland Eddy (*The Cats of Africa*, 1968), "there are people scattered over the world who are willing to argue the rights of animals against the rights of humans."

As an example, take biologist Jesus Garzon ("Suso"), who for years led a battle to publicize and protect a wild area of Spain known as Monfrague, home to lynx and wild cats as well as numerous other species. His single-handed lobbying efforts resulted in the establishment of Monfrague Natural Park in 1979.

Similarly, American field biologist Alan

Rabinowitz initiated a study of jaguars and other wild felid species in the Cockscomb Basin of Belize. The results of his research gained international attention and contributed to the establishment of the world's first jaguar sanctuary.

In 1968, when a South African farmer gave Ann van Dyk a pair of orphaned cheetah cubs, this simple event changed her life. She ended up converting her 296-acre chicken farm near Pretoria into the De Wildt Cheetah Research Center, a private breeding facility for cheetahs and other endangered mammals. Cheetahs are notoriously difficult to breed in captivity, but van Dyk pioneered new techniques that proved successful. In 1975 six females produced a record twenty-three cubs. Since then more than four hundred cheetah cubs have been born there.

In Seattle Helen Freeman turned her fascination with snow leopards and her captive studies of these endangered cats at the Woodland Park Zoo into the International Snow Leopard Trust. Since its founding in 1981, the ISLT has supported conservation efforts in central Asia through education programs, research, training, technical assistance, and technology transfer, sponsored snow leopard field research projects in India and Nepal, and developed an interactive database called the Snow Leopard Information Management System (SLIMS).

For the past twenty-eight years, Pat Quillen has single-handedly raised small endangered cats on her property near San Diego, California. Pat is known for her success at breeding and maintaining small felid species that are difficult to keep in captivity. Working with the São Paulo Zoo in Brazil, she is now sharing her knowledge on felid breeding behavior and management to help establish cooperative captive breeding programs for jaguarundi, margay, oncilla, and pampas cats in their country of origin.

In 1986, Bill Yeates organized a group of California conservationists into the nonprofit Mountain Lion Foundation based in Sacramento. Their goal was to get legislation passed to stop cougar trophy hunting. Through effective lobbying and fund-raising efforts, they succeeded in getting the California Wildlife Protection Act, Proposition 117, on the ballot and passed in June 1990. The Act permanently bans trophy hunting of mountain lions and provides $30 million annually through the year 2020 to acquire and enhance California's wildlife habitat. The Foundation is now lobbying to gain greater protection for the state's bobcats and black bears.

In India, Billy Arjan Singh converted his own farm into a private tiger sanctuary run by the Tiger Haven Wildlife Trust, then battled for ten years to establish a sanctuary for India's endangered barashingha, or swamp deer. When the Indian government delayed signing the documents necessary to establish Dudwa National Park, Billy used elephants to rustle up the deer and drive them onto the government-owned land. To provide the deer with food, he illegally plowed several acres and planted it with millet. His efforts resulted in a new park which helped save half the world's population of swamp deer— as well as fifty more tigers.

Under the tough anti-poaching policies of Fateh Singh Rathore, India's field director for the Ranthambhore Tiger Reserve, tigers increased from fourteen to forty in thirteen years. Because his strong presence meant uncompromised protection for the park and its wildlife, Rathore was once attacked by angry herdsmen who broke his arm, shattered his kneecap, beat him unconscious, and left him for dead, with injuries that sent him to the hospital for three months. For that, and his tireless efforts to protect Ranthambhore's wildlife, he was awarded India's highest civilian medal for valor—twice.

In January 1990 Michael (Tiger Mike) Day traveled to Thailand to film the elusive Indo-Chinese tiger. When his favorite tiger, "The Big Boy," was shot by poachers, he responded by setting up The Tiger Trust in England to attract international support for tiger conservation, and built a natural habitat enclosure for tigers seized in illegal commerce.

Worldwide it is possible to find individuals who are involved in the conservation of wild cats and their habitats. One person *can* make a difference. Collectively such individuals can turn a whisper into a conservation roar.

WHAT YOU CAN DO

From energy and water conservation to waste reduction and recycled disposal, there are many ways to help save wildlife and wild habitats:

• If you own a cat (or dog), have it altered to prevent unwanted offspring.

• To help reduce pressure on tropical rain forests, buy wood and wood products made from trees that are commercially farmed.

To preserve the fragile, high-altitude habitat of the endangered snow leopard (*Panthera uncia*), twelve different countries are now working together in an international conservation effort.

- To attract birds and other wildlife to your property, plant fruit and nut trees. Provide additional nesting boxes and roosts, if needed.
- If you own land, retain existing wildlife corridors, or create new ones that will allow animals to move across your property freely.
- To attract wildlife and keep your community green, plant native trees wherever possible.
- Join organizations that are working on conservation issues that are important to you, and volunteer your time or dollars to help.
- Contact your state wildlife or game department and find out what is being done to protect native animals.
- Keep an eye out for polluters, private or industrial, and report them.
- Contact your elected representatives about environmental issues that are of concern to you. Make your viewpoint known; propose solutions.
- Start a conservation club.
- Most important, support laws that prohibit the sale and trade of endangered plants and animals, and the products made from them: fur coats, trophies, body-part souvenirs, beauty aids, and Asian medicinal products.

The following organizations provide free fact sheets and brochures that explain the laws to protect wildlife:

The U.S. Fish and Wildlife Service
U.S. Department of the Interior
Washington, DC 20240

U.S. Customs Service
1301 Constitution Avenue NW
Washington, DC 20229

U.S. Department of Agriculture
APHIS PPQ
Federal Building
6505 Belcrest Road
Hyattsville, MD 20782

TRAFFIC (USA)
1250 24th Street NW
Washington, DC 20037

HOW TO SEE CATS IN THE WILD

Opportunities exist to see cats in the wild: trips to photograph bobcats; safaris to see lions, leopards, and tigers in the best wildlife parks of Africa and Asia; hands-on field research expeditions to study cougars in Idaho. The following organizations can help make it happen:

Abercrombie & Kent International
1520 Kensington Road
Oak Brook, IL 60521

Adventure Center
1311 63rd St., Suite 200
Emeryville, CA 94608

Earthwatch
680 Mount Auburn Street
Watertown, MA 02272-9104

Forum International
91 Gregory Lane
Pleasant Hill, CA 94523

Himalayan Travel, Inc.
112 Prospect Street
Stamford, CT 06901

International Expeditions
One Environs Parks
Helena, AL 35080

International Zoological Expeditions
210 Washington Street
Sherborn, MA 01770

Journeys
4011B Jackson
Ann Arbor, MI 48103

Mountain Travel/Sobek Expeditions
6420 Fairmont Avenue
El Cerrito, CA 94530

Nature Expeditions International
P.O. Box 11496
Eugene, OR 97440

Overseas Adventure Travel
349 Broadway
Cambridge, MA 02139

Questers
Worldwide Nature Tours
275 Park Avenue South
New York, NY 10010

Sierra Club
Outings Department
730 Polk Street
San Francisco, CA 94109

Smithsonian Research Expeditions
490 L'Enfant Plaza SW
Washington, DC 20560

Wildlands Studies
San Francisco State University
3 Mosswood Circle
Cazadero, CA 95421

WHERE TO WRITE TO HELP WILD CATS

American Zoo and Aquarium
  Association
7970-D Old Georgetown Road
Bethesda, MD 70814
301/907-7777

Hornocker Wildlife Research Institute
University of Idaho
P.O. Box 3246
Moscow, ID 83843
208/885-6859

The Nature Conservancy
1800 N. Kent Street
Arlington, VA 22209
800/628-6860

The National Wildlife Federation
8925 Leesburg Pike
Vienna, VA 22184
703/790-4000
800/432-6564

Considered the world's smallest feline, the rusty-spotted cat (*Felis rubiginosa*) is but one of thirty-seven magnificent species of wild cats that inhabit the planet. They are one of the tiniest living members of a long line of extremely successful carnivores—the *Felidae*.

The Wilderness Society
900 17th Street NW
Washington, DC 20006-2596

The Sierra Club
730 Polk Street
San Francisco, CA 94109
415/776-2211

The National Parks and Conservation
  Association
1776 Massachusetts Avenue NW
Washington, DC 20036
800/NAT-PARKS

The Wildlife Conservation Society
185th & Southern Avenue
Bronx, NY 10460
718/220-5l97

Defenders of Wildlife
1101 14th Street NW, Suite 1400
Washington, DC 20005
202/682-9400

The World Wildlife Fund
1250 24th Street NW, Suite 400
Washington, DC 20037
202/293-4800

U.S. Fish and Wildlife Service
Refuges and Wildlife
1849 C Street NW
Washington, DC 20240
703/358-1769

Jersey Wildlife Preservation Trust
Les Augres Manor
Trinity, Jersey

Channel Islands JE3 5BF
British Isles
011-44-534-864666

International Snow Leopard Trust
4649 Sunnyside Avenue North
Seattle, WA 98l03
206/634-2421

International Society For Endangered
  Cats (Canada) Inc.
124 Lynnbrook Road SE
Calgary, Alberta T2C 1S6
403/279-5892

The Mountain Lion Foundation
P.O. Box l896
Sacramento, CA 95812
916/442-266

Bibliography

Allen, Durward. *Our Wildlife Legacy.* New York: Funk and Wagnall, 1954.

Badino, G. *Big Cats of the World.* New York: Crown Publishers, 1975.

Brett, C. *Wild Cats.* New York: Dorset Press, 1992

Brown, L., C. Flavin, and S. Postel. *Saving the Planet.* New York: W. W. Norton & Co., 1974.

Brucker, D.J.R. *Van der Steen's Cats.* New York: Fromm International Publishing Corp., 1984.

Burton, J. (ed.). *The Atlas of Endangered Species.* New York: Macmillan Publishers, 1991.

Burton, R. (ed.). *Animal Life.* New York: Oxford University Press, 1991.

Call, M. C. *Cougar: Ghost of the Rockies.* San Francisco: Sierra Club, 1993.

Capstick, P. H. *Maneaters.* Los Angeles: Petersen Publishing Co., 1981.

Caras, Roger A. *A Cat Is Watching.* New York: Simon and Schuster, 1990.

————. *Panther!* Lincoln, Neb.: Lincoln University Press, 1990.

————. *A Celebration of Cats.* New York: Simon and Schuster, 1986.

Cole, Joanna. *A Cat's Body.* New York: William Morrow & Co., 1982.

Corbett, J. *Man-Eaters of Kumaon.* New York: Oxford University Press, 1946.

Eaton, Randall L. (ed.). *The World's Cats.* Volume I: Ecology and Conservation. Winston, Ore.: World Wildlife Safari, 1973.

————. *The World's Cats.* Volume II: Biology, Behavior and Management of Reproduction. Seattle: Feline Research Group, Woodland Park Zoo, 1974.

————. *The World's Cats.* Volume III, No. l: Contributions to Status, Management and Conservation. Seattle: Department of Zoology, University of Washington, 1976.

————. *The World's Cats.* Volume III, No. 2: Contributions to Biology, Ecology, Behavior and Evolution. Seattle: Burke Museum, 1976.

Edey, Maitland. *The Cats of Africa.* New York: Time-Life Books, l968.

Eisenberg, J. F. *Mammals of the Neotropics. The Northern Neotropics.* Vol. I. Chicago: University of Chicago Press, 1989.

Ewer, R. F. *The Carnivores.* Ithaca, N.Y.: Comstock Publishing Associates, 1973.

Fagen, R. *Animal Play Behavior.* Oxford: Oxford University Press, 1981.

Guggisberg, C.A.W. *Wild Cats of the World.* New York: Taplinger Publishing Company, 1975.

Hazen, R., and J. Trefil. *Science Matters: Achieving Scientific Literacy.* New York: Doubleday & Co., 1991.

Hofer, Angelika, and Gunter Ziesler. *The Lion Family Book.* Salsburg, Austria: Verlag Neugebauer Press, 1988.

Opposite: The "king of beasts," a majestic lion (*Panthera leo*) glows in the late-day sun. Felines represent the highest level in the evolution of carnivores. As stalking, hunting meat-eaters, they are the nearest thing to predatory perfection.

Kitchener, A. *The Natural History of the Wild Cats.* Ithaca, N.Y.: Comstock Publishing Associates, 1991.

Leyhausen, Paul. *Cat Behavior: The Predatory and Social Behavior of Domestic and Wild Cats.* New York: Garland STPM Press, 1979.

Loxton, H. *The Noble Cat: Aristocrat of the Animal World.* New York: Portland House, 1990.

Matthiessen, P. *Shadows of Africa.* New York: Harry Abrams, 1992.

McBride, Chris. *The White Lions of Timbavati.* New York: Paddington Press, Ltd., 1977.

McDougal, C. *The Face of the Tiger.* London: Rivington Books, 1977.

Myers, N. *The Sinking Ark: A New Look at the Problem of Disappearing Species.* New York: Pergamon Press, 1979.

National Wildlife Federation. *Kingdom of Cats.* Washington, D.C.: National Wildlife Federation, 1987.

Natoli, E. *Cats of the World.* New York: Crescent Books, 1987.

Neff, N. A. *The Big Cats: The Paintings of Guy Coheleach.* New York: Abradale Press, 1982.

Newman, A. *Tropical Rainforest.* New York: Facts on File, 1990.

Overbeck, Cynthia. *Lions.* Minneapolis: Lerner Publications Co., 1981.

Owens, M., and D. Owens. *Cry of the Kalahari.* Boston: Houghton Mifflin, 1984.

Pugnetti, G. *Simon & Schuster's Guide to Cats.* New York: Simon & Schuster, 1983.

Rabinowitz, A. *Jaguar.* New York: Arbor House, 1986.

———. *Chasing the Dragon's Tail.* New York: Doubleday & Co., 1991.

Ricciuti, E. R. *The Wild Cats.* New York: Ridge Press, 1979.

Rogers, B. R. *Big Cats.* New York: Gallery Books, 1991.

Ryden, H. *Your Cat's Wild Cousins.* New York: Lodestar Books, Dutton, 1991.

———. *Bobcat Year.* New York: Lyons & Burford, 1981.

Schaller, G. B. *The Deer and the Tiger: A Study of Wildlife in India.* Chicago: University of Chicago Press, 1967.

———. *The Serengeti Lion.* Chicago: University of Chicago Press, 1972.

Schueler, D. *Incident at Eagle Ranch: Predators as Prey in the American West.* Tucson: University of Arizona Press, 1991.

Seidensticker, John, and Susan Lumpkin. *Great Cats: Majestic Creatures of the Wild.* Emmaus, Pennsylvania: Rodale Press, 1991.

Silvester, John, and Anne Mobbs. *A Catland Companion.* New York: Summit Books, 1991.

Simon, Seymour. *Big Cats.* New York: HarperCollins, 1991.

Singh, A. *Tiger! Tiger!* London: Jonathan Cape, 1984.

Sunquist, F., and M. Sunquist. *Tiger Moon.* Chicago: University of Chicago Press, 1988.

Thapar, Valmik. *Tigers: The Secret Life.* Emmaus, PA: Rodale Press, 1989.

Tilson, R. L., and U. S. Seal. *Tigers of the World.* Park Ridge, N.J.: Noyes Publications, 1987.

Turbak, G. *America's Great Cats.* Flagstaff, Ariz.: Northland Publishing, 1986.

Wildt, D. E., J. D. Mellen, and U. S. Seal. *Felid Action Plan, 1991 and 1992:* AAZPA Felid Taxon Advisory Group Regional Collection Plan and IUCN Captive Breeding Specialist Group Global Felid Action Plan. Washington, D.C.: American Association of Zoological Parks and Aquariums, 1992.

Wilson, E. O. (ed.). *Biodiversity.* Washington, D.C.: National Academy Press, 1988.

Acknowledgments

Many people are involved in one way or another in the production of a book of this kind, and I have been most fortunate to have had assistance from many sources. First and foremost, I wish to express my appreciation to the many people who helped with arrangements to access these beautiful animals, and to the biologists, naturalists, and wildlife specialists who have supplied me personally with information about the cats in their parts of the world. I thank the following contributors: Pat Quillen, SOS Care, Inc.; Bill and Penny Andrews; Bernard Harrison, Singapore Zoological Gardens; Susan Mallard, San Diego Wild Animal Park; Pat Callahan, Cincinnati Zoo and Botanical Garden; Karen Sausman, Living Desert Reserve; Gary Stolz, U.S. Fish and Wildlife Service; Mike Lockyer, Nick Marx, Hazel Burton, Terry Whittaker, Howletts/Port Lymphne Estates; Ann van Dyk, De Wildt Cheetah Research Center, South Africa; Tungku Nazim, Zoo Negara, Malaysia; Dr. Faical Simon, São Paulo Zoo, Brazil; Dr. Luis Gonzales Providel, Santiago, Chile; Dr. A. M. Saliba, São Paulo, Brazil; Troy and Kirsten Hyde; Shirley Bonekemper, Cincinnati Zoo; Linda Corcoran, Bronx Zoo; Eduardo Nycander, Rainforest Expeditions.

And special thanks go to Mel Calvan, Christine Eckhoff, Ray Pfortner, and Deirdre Skillman of Art Wolfe, Inc.

—ART WOLFE

I would like to give special thanks to the following individuals who helped make this project possible: Pat Quillen of SOS Care, Inc., for her humor, encouragement, and insight into the wonders of wild cats; Helen Freeman of the International Snow Leopard Trust for her friendship and inspiration as a conservation role model; Alan Rabinowitz of the Wildlife Conservation Society for help reviewing the manuscript and the friendship of a kindred spirit; Warren Kinzey for the ecological insight gained while exploring the rain forests of South America together; and Michael Hutchins, Betsy Dressler, Stephen O'Brien, Ken Goddard, and Howard Quigley for invaluable help with facts.

I'd like to thank Art Wolfe for creating such beautiful cat photographs and for the opportunity to write this book; hard-working Christine Eckhoff, Deirdre Skillman, Mel Calvan, and Ray Pfortner for their attention to the endless detail needed to complete this project; and Gary Stolz of the U.S. Fish and Wildlife Service, for helpful review and comment.

Special thanks go to Mike Konecny for sharing Belize's Cockscomb Basin and his fascination with wild cats; editor Joni Praded of *Animals* magazine for the assignments on wild cats that helped lead to this book; cat-lover Ken Brooker for references and encouragement; Caden Gray for artistic inspiration; the Feral Housewives for spirit-revival in the Grand Canyon; Michelle Lindsley for her workaholic empathy; Carol Fahrenbruch for a lifetime of friendship and mental nutrition; Tom Boyden and George Schnibbe for humor adjustments; and Bob Citron for the child-care needed to finish this book.

Last but not least, I give heartfelt thanks to my parents Norma and Bill Sleeper, and siblings Bill and Lynne Sleeper for their "all in the family" encouragement and support; to Bugs, my fourteen-year-old Burmese house cat for invaluable tips on felid behavior and unfaltering companionship during preparation of the manuscript; and to my three very patient, animal-loving children, Kelly, David, and Josh, who finally gave up asking, "Are you done with the cat book yet?"

Art and I would both like to thank senior editor Brandt Aymar, production editor Mark McCauslin, designer Lauren Dong, production supervisor Bill Peabody, and marketing specialist Patty Eddy of Crown Publishers for contributing their unique talents to *Wild Cats of the World*.

—BARBARA SLEEPER

Index